LANDS OF THE EARLY CHRISTIAN STORY

1583

CAPPADOCIA

• Tarsus

CYPRUS

Salami

• Iconium
• Lystra

Paphos

Tyre

Caesarea

Attalia

ASIA

Ephesus

Miletus

Myra

Troas

Rhodes

CRETE

Lasea

MEDITERRANEAN SEA

Alexandria

EGYPT

Philippi

MACEDONIA

Thessalonica

Athens

Corinth

GREECE

Beroea

500

250

0 km

ITALY

Rome

Syracuse

SICILY

MALTA

CYRENAICA

AFRICA

AND ITS BACKGROUND   Book Five

Jesus
the Nazarene

NORMAN J. BULL, M.A., Ph.D.

Illustrated by Grace Golden, A.R.C.A.

HULTON EDUCATIONAL PUBLICATIONS

Titles in this series

OLD TESTAMENT TITLES

Book One   Founders of the Jews
Book Two   Kings of the Jews
Book Three   Prophets of the Jews
Book Four   The Church of the Jews

NEW TESTAMENT TITLES

Book Five   Jesus the Nazarene
Book Six   The Parables of Jesus
Book Seven   The Church of Jesus Begins
Book Eight   The Church of Jesus Grows

© NORMAN BULL 1968
ISBN 0 7175 0981 8

First published 1968 by Hulton Educational Publications Ltd.,
Raans Road, Amersham, Bucks.
Reprinted 1971, 1972, 1973, 1976, 1977, 1979
2nd Edition 1982
Printed in the German Democratic Republic

Contents

The land of Jesus   7

Nazareth   53

Galilee   91

Jerusalem   135

Index   185

Mt. Carmel

Mt. Herme
Sea of Galile

Galilee

Samar

Bethlehem
in Judaea

Qumra
Dead S

The Jordan

PALESTINE IN THE
TIME OF CHRIST

a scale comparision

0 km   75   150

Mediterranean Sea

GALI-
LEE   S. of Galilee

SAMARIA   R. Jordan

JUDAEA   Dead
Sea

The land of Jesus

Palestine

The land of Jesus lies at the eastern end of the Mediterranean Sea. It is often called THE HOLY LAND because Jesus lived there. It has other names, too.

In very ancient times it had been called CANAAN which means LAND OF PURPLE. This was because the country was famous for its rare and precious purple dye, made from shell-fish gathered on the sea shore.

Later, when the Jewish tribes conquered Canaan they gave it a new name—ISRAEL which means MAY GOD RULE. This has always been the Jews' name for Palestine. When the Jews won back their country in 1948, and set up their own State, they naturally called it ISRAEL. The proclamation of the new State said: "Israel was the birthplace of the Jewish people."

The most common name for the land of Jesus is PALESTINE, and this is the one we shall use. It comes from "Philistine". A thousand years before the time of Jesus the Philistines had been powerful enemies of the Jews. They nearly won the whole country before King David defeated them. That was why the Greeks called it "Palaistine"—"Land of the Philistines". In the Roman language this became "Palestina", and from it came our word PALESTINE.

The land of Jesus lies between the Mediterranean Sea and the River Jordan. It is a very small country, about the size of Wales or

Belgium. It is 80 km wide from west to east. It is about 240 km long from Dan in the north to Beersheba in the south—"from Land's End to John O'Groats", as we would say.

The coastal plain

Although Palestine is a small country it has many differences in geography and climate. We can divide it into four main parts and see how they differ.

If you look at the top of the map and follow the coast of the Mediterranean Sea southwards you will see that a flat plain runs all along it. In the north is the narrow coastal strip which used to be the land of the Phoenician people, with their great cities of Tyre and Sidon. Mount Carmel, a sacred range of hills rises to 5,400 m and cuts into the coastal plain. South of Carmel is the Plain of Sharon, famous in Bible times for its oak forests and its lovely spring carpet of wild flowers. South of Sharon is the Plain of Philistia where the Philistines settled. After their defeat by King David, they were confined to this coastal plain.

There were no natural harbours along the coast of Palestine and this may help to explain why the Jews never became sailors. Small ports were made at Joppa and Caesarea for the coastal trading ships and the Roman galleys, with their shallow draught, which brought troops and merchandise to Palestine. The Jews of the coastal plain lived mainly by agriculture, growing rich crops in the fertile soil.

The central mountains

The second part of Palestine, going inland from the coastal plain, is

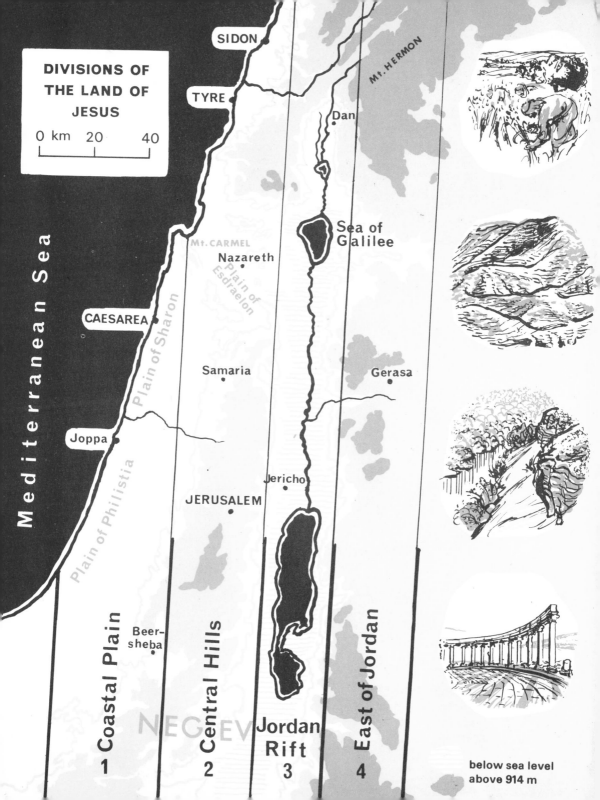

DIVISIONS OF THE LAND OF JESUS

0 km   20   40

Mediterranean Sea

SIDON

TYRE

Mt. HERMON

Dan

Mt. CARMEL

Nazareth

Plain of Esdraelon

Sea of Galilee

CAESAREA

Plain of Sharon

Samaria

Gerasa

Joppa

Plain of Philistia

Jericho

JERUSALEM

Beer-sheba

NEGEV

Coastal Plain
1

Central Hills
2

Jordan Rift
3

East of Jordan
4

below sea level
above 914 m

a long range of mountains. It is the backbone of Palestine. In the north are the hundred hills of Galilee, watered by the streams flowing down from the mountains of Lebanon. They are separated from the hills of the south by the wide plain of Esdraelon, which runs right across the country from the Mediterranean Sea to the River Jordan. ESDRAELON means GOD SOWS—a fine name for this rich and fertile plain.

South of Esdraelon rise the hills of Samaria, with olive groves on the slopes and cornfields in the valleys. Then, south of Samaria, the hills of Judaea rise higher still. They form a plateau of grey limestone where little can be grown, except on terraces made like shelves on the hill-sides. But the grass made fodder for sheep, and all through Bible times shepherding was the main occupation of the men of the hill-country of Judaea.

South of Judaea the hills fall away to the flat desert called the NEGEB—the DRY, or the SOUTH COUNTRY.

ROMAN ROADS All over their Empire the Romans built wonderful roads. In Britain some of the roads still follow the old Roman roads of ancient Britain.

On the left is a road in Palestine today, built by the Romans between the cities of Aleppo and Antioch in Syria, the country north of Palestine. Roads in Galilee were not so well made or maintained, but milestones were set up on main roads.

Trade routes

As we would expect, the main road through Palestine ran along the coastal plain. It was called THE WAY OF THE SOUTH. From Egypt in the south it ran up the coastal plain, skirted Mount Carmel, and then crossed the Plain of Esdraelon. At the Sea of Galilee it joined another famous Roman road called THE WAY OF THE SEA, with branch roads leading north and east.

Thus, although Palestine was a small country, it was an important one, for the great trade route between the East and the West ran through it. Many an army marched along it in Bible times. Many a battle was fought in the Plain of Esdraelon.

When Jesus was a boy he would often climb the hills near Nazareth, his home town. From them he could look down on the busy Roman roads. He would see Roman soldiers, travelling merchants, camel trains laden with goods, lords and ladies, rich men and beggars, pilgrims and vagabonds.

The River Jordan

The third main part of the land of Jesus was the valley of the Jordan. The River Jordan was formed when a great crack was made in the earth in very ancient times as the world cooled. This crack made a deep rift or opening in the earth which naturally became filled with water. You can follow it on your map from north to south. In Palestine it includes the Sea of Galilee, the River Jordan and the Dead Sea. Then it runs on south through the desert down into Africa where it forms the Red Sea, Lake Tanganyika and Lake Nyasa. This great rift in the earth has been called "the deepest ditch in the world".

The main source of the River Jordan is Mount Hermon in the north. This majestic mountain, nearly 32 km long and 2,700 m at its highest peak, is capped with snow all the year round. Its waters form LAKE HULEH, called in the Bible THE WATERS OF MEROM, which is about four miles long. Its marshy waters were the home of various wildfowl and paper was made from its papyrus reeds.

From Lake Huleh the River Jordan flows south for 16 km, dropping all the way, till it reaches the SEA OF GALILEE. This is really an inland lake, but it was called "Sea" because of its great size—some 20 km long and 12 km wide. Sometimes in the Gospels it is called the "Sea of Tiberias" or "Lake Gennesaret"; sometimes it

12

DIVISIONS OF THE LAND OF JESUS

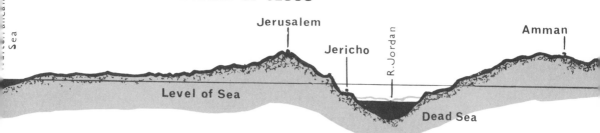

COASTAL PLAIN   CENTRAL HILLS   JORDAN RIFT   EAST OF JORDAN

Here is the land of Jesus looked at another way, from west to east. It shows the four main divisions of the country clearly. It also shows what great differences there are in the geography of Palestine.

The Dead Sea lies 392 m below sea level; its depth is 365 m. It is the lowest stretch of water in the world.

The hills, on the other hand, rise to a great height. Mount Hermon is 274 m high. Jerusalem itself is 792 m above sea level, Nazareth 335 m.

is simply called "the lake" or "the sea". A very poetic name for it was "Chinnereth" meaning "Shaped like a Harp". It was full of fish and its shores were dotted with fishing villages. Jesus called some of its fishermen to be his disciples.

The name JORDAN means "down-rusher"—a good name for the river as it goes on down from the Sea of Galilee to the Dead Sea. The distance is 104 km, but the River Jordan twists and turns like a snake for 354 km. The valley it flows through is the deepest in the world. In Bible times there was a thick sub-tropical jungle along its banks—the home then of such beasts as lions and bears.

13

When the river enters the Dead Sea it is about 400 metres below the level of the sea. Not even canoes could stay afloat in its swirling currents. People crossed it by fords; there were no bridges till the methodical Romans built them. It was in these waters that Jesus was baptised by his cousin John.

The Dead Sea, too, is really a lake, not a sea. But there is no doubt about its being dead. Nothing can live in its waters for they are full of minerals and five times more salt than the oceans. If you dive into it, you bob up like a cork for you cannot sink. People have been photographed lying in the Dead Sea reading a newspaper. Streams flow into it but the fierce heat of the sun quickly evaporates their waters. The Dead Sea is 75 km long and 16 km at its greatest width.

The land around the Dead Sea is dry and hot and barren. Men like John the Baptist lived a life of solitude in this wilderness. Jesus came here to be alone with God before he began his ministry.

East of Jordan

The fourth part of the land of Jesus was the country east of the River Jordan—today called "Trans-Jordan". It is a plateau of high land split up by streams.

Jews had lived there as wandering nomads in Old Testament times, grazing sheep and goats. But the land belonged to foreign tribes and the Jews never really settled there.

In the time of Jesus there were nine Greek cities on the east of the River Jordan, and one on the west of the river called Bethshan. These ten cities formed a league to keep out the desert tribes. This was called the DECAPOLIS from Greek words meaning THE TEN

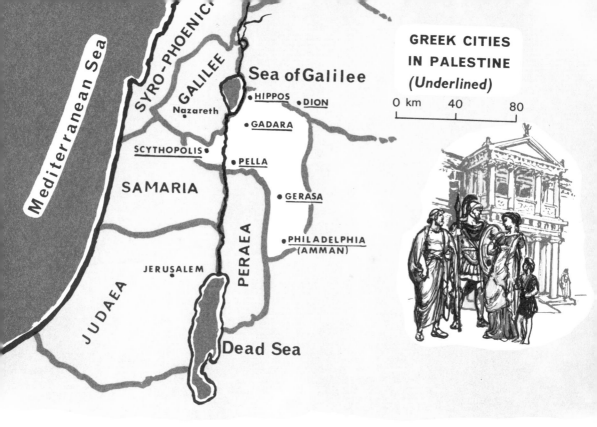

There were Greek cities in Palestine in the time of Jesus. They joined to-gether in a league called the DECAPOLIS or TEN CITIES.

But there were as many as 18 towns in the league. All of them were on the east of the Jordan, except for Scythopolis on the west.

The people of these cities followed Greek customs and gods. To the Jews they were pagans. But Jews did visit these towns and some Jewish traders lived in them.

We are not told that Jesus ever visited these towns but he did travel in their territory. Look up and read: Matthew 8.28; Mark 5.1.

CITIES. One of them is today Amman, the capital of the kingdom of Jordan. Another has been dug up by archaeologists. It was called Gerasa or Jerash and from its fine ruins we can see what these Greek cities were like. They had hippodromes for horse-racing and theatres for plays. The people followed Greek customs and worshipped the Greek gods.

To the Jews these were pagan cities. But they knew of them and some Jews visited them. Jesus travelled near two of them—Gadara and Gerasa.

There were other pagan cities, west of Jordan, in the land of

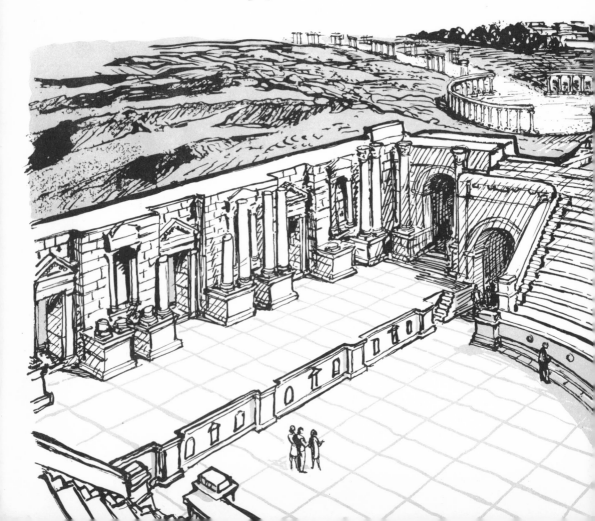

Jesus. Among those mentioned in the story of Jesus are Samaria, Tiberias and Caesarea Philippi. About 6 km from Nazareth in Galilee, where Jesus grew up, was another pagan city named Sepphoris.

We cannot be sure that Jesus went into these towns or that he deliberately avoided them. But he certainly travelled near them and he gladly helped people from them. Jesus may well have spoken their Greek language—as well as the Hebrew language in which the Jewish Scriptures were written, and the Aramaic language spoken by the Jews in Palestine.

GERASA Here are the ruins of Gerasa, now called Jerash, one of the Graeco-Roman cities of the Decapolis. These ruins date from the 2nd century A.D., when the Roman city was at the height of its prosperity. Its walls were about three miles round. The city was entered through a Triumphal Arch. Here you can see the theatre—some of its seats are still numbered. In the distance is the Forum, a kind of market-place, oval in shape. Beyond that is the Street of Columns, the main shopping street. It had 520 stone columns lining it, of which 75 still remain.

Gerasa also had fine Roman temples to the Greek gods, Zeus and Artemis; a hippodrome for horse races, seating 15,000 people; baths; and a stadium for sports and athletics. Orange and pink granite was used for all these wonderful buildings.

Read Mark 5. 1.

Roman rule

In the time of Jesus Palestine was part of the mighty Roman Empire. It included most of Europe, though Britain was not conquered till a few years after his earthly life. Roman rule was good if conquered peoples submitted to it. It gave them peace and order, good laws, stern but fair justice, fine roads, well-built cities and easy communications with other lands.

18

THE ROMAN EMPIRE AT THE TIME OF JESUS

ASIA

PARTHIAN EMPIRE

SYRIA

...usalem

These are the heads of
the two emperors under
whom Jesus lived.

Emperor Augustus,
29 B.C. to A.D. 14
(from a cameo)

Emperor Tiberius,
A.D. 14-37
(from a statue)

The Jews never really submitted to Roman rule. No people like having their country occupied by foreign troops. The Jews, who loved freedom and independence, hated it.

But there were deeper reasons. The Romans, who already had their own pagan gods, took over even more gods from the countries they won. One religion was much the same as another to them. But each religion had to be approved and licensed, and its worshippers

19

had to obey Roman laws. Conquered peoples had to offer worship to the Emperor, too. Religion was controlled by the State.

ROMAN RELIGION

The Romans worshipped many gods and goddesses. This ancient Roman bowl was found in Germany. It is made of silver, overlaid with gold. The figure is of Roma, the goddess of the city of Rome.

This painting from the third century A.D. shows Roman soldiers giving worship to their gods. They are led by the officer on the left who is burning incense.

With the Jews it was just the opposite. They believed in the one and only true God. He was their ruler and their laws came from him. They must obey his laws, not those of men. They could never worship a mere human being, even if he was the Emperor of the world. Their State was controlled by religion.

The Romans tried hard to keep the peace in Palestine and not to offend the Jews, but they could never succeed.

Roman taxation

Nothing angered the Jews more than Roman taxation. Every people conquered by Rome had to pay for Roman rule. They had to do military service and to pay taxes. The Jews refused to fight for Rome and they were not forced to serve as soldiers, but they had to pay all the Roman taxes.

Part of the trouble was that the Jews already paid one form of tax as a religious duty. These religious dues were of two kinds. One was the Temple Tax which every Jew had to pay to the Temple each year before the Passover Feast. In the time of Jesus it was a didrachma—a coin worth about one pound, quite a sum for a poor peasant. The other religious duty was to give a TITHE or TENTH of everything grown on one's land. For the land belonged to God, it had been given by him, and this was a natural way of thanking him. Herds, flocks, crops, fruits, even herbs from the garden and eggs from the chickens—everything had to be tithed. The "first-fruits" of barley and wheat, of vines and figs, of pomegranates and olives and of honey—all these were given to God. No good Jew would think of neglecting such duties, even if he found them a burden.

In the Ten Commandments of Moses the Jews were forbidden to make any graven images. They were so careful not to break this law that they would not make coins. At first they exchanged goods by barter. Then they used gold and silver for buying and selling, measuring them by weight (Genesis 23.16). Gold was worth 15 times more than silver.

Later they used the coins of other lands, Phoenicia, Greece and Rome. About 150 B.C. they began to make their own coins. But even then they avoided using images on their coins. Instead, they had designs of fruit or corn, olive or palm branches, or the sacred candlesticks of the Temple.

The coins pictured here are shekels made about 130 A.D. The shekel was an old Babylonian measure of weight. The Jews adopted it, and the silver shekel became their most common coin.

Left: "Holy Jerusalem"
Right: "Shekel of Israel, 1st year"

Left: "Holy Jerusalem"
Right: "Shekel of Israel, 2nd year"

The Temple Tax had to be paid in this money. Traditionally it was a half-shekel, but it could be paid in the Greek silver coin called a didrachma which was of the same value (Matthew 17.24).

The years referred to are from 132 to 135 A.D. when the Jews rebelled against Rome and claimed to be a free people. When at last the Romans defeated them they were expelled from Palestine altogether.

LAND OF JESUS

The Roman silver denarius

Roman taxes had to be paid in Roman money. The most common Roman coin was this silver denarius. It is translated as a "penny" in the Old English Bible. Although it may sound very little, money was different then and it was a day's wage for a labourer (Matthew 20.2), and enough to keep a man for a day (Luke 10.35). The Jews paid Roman taxes in this coin (Mark 12.15). This is a denarius of the Emperor Tiberius (14-37 A.D.) under whom Jesus lived. Around his image are the words "Tiberius, Caesar Augustus, son of the divine Augustus", and his head is wreathed in laurel. The figure on the other side is symbolic. Around it are the words "Chief Pontiff"— that is, "High Priest".

Coins often had bits chipped off. The tax-collectors weighed them to make sure. Some of our coins have milled edges to prevent this.

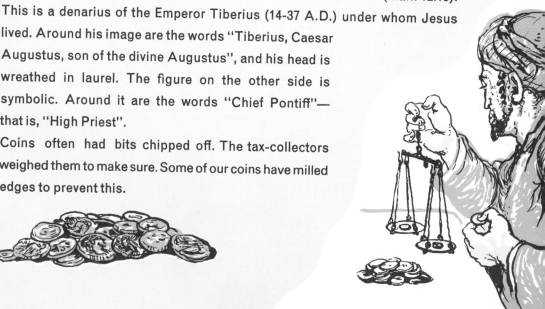

On top of this the Jews had to pay taxes to Rome, so that they were taxed twice over. Roman taxes were of two kinds. First were direct taxes, collected by the Roman authorities themselves. There was one on land and it amounted to nearly a quarter of what the land produced. There was another on a man's money, the amount depending upon his wealth.

Indirect taxes were rather like our customs duties, but the Romans did not collect these themselves. Every five years the right to collect taxes was auctioned at Rome. It was given to the man who made the highest bid. He was out to make a good profit, of course. He hired local men to collect the taxes for him, and they too had to make their profit. Thus everyone cheated under this dreadful system of collecting taxes.

The local tax-collectors were called "publicani" in Latin, the language of the Romans. That is why they are called "publicans" in our old English Bible. These tax-collectors sat in their customs-houses throughout Palestine in the time of Jesus. In the market-place, at the cross-roads, and by the bridge the tax-collector would be waiting with, perhaps, a Roman soldier standing by.

The Jews hated paying taxes to Rome. They hated being cheated. They hated most of all the traitor Jews who collected the taxes for the Romans. "Tax collectors" are always linked with "sinners" in the Gospels. They were outcasts of Jewish society, rich in their ill-gotten wealth, but poor in friends.

Yet not all tax collectors were evil men. One of them, named Matthew Levi, collected taxes at the fishing town of Capernaum. Jesus called him as he sat in the customs-house, and he became one of the twelve apostles. Another we read about was Zacchaeus, the chief tax-collector at the important city of Jericho. He became a disciple of Jesus.

One of the stories Jesus told was about two men who both prayed to God—a religious man who boasted to God of his goodness, and a tax-collector who humbly admitted his sins. It was the tax-collector, Jesus said, who was forgiven by God.

Rulers in Palestine

Palestine had become part of the Roman Empire in 63 B.C. There had been civil war among the Jews, and one of the rival groups had appealed to a Roman general named Pompey to help them. He came to Jerusalem with his soldiers and took it in the name of Rome. Pompey was curious to find out about the famous God of the Jews. With his sword in his hand he marched into the most sacred part of the Temple—the "Holy of Holies". He thought he would find a glittering idol there. But the chamber was dark—and quite empty.

The Romans needed rulers for their new conquest. They soon found how difficult it was to control the Jews. They put Jewish leaders in power but there was constant civil war. Then they found the ruler they needed in a man named Herod. He was a desert sheikh from the land of Edom or Idumea, south of the Dead Sea. Herod was a clever politician, a ruthless soldier and a strong ruler. He won the friendship of Rome and was always loyal to its rulers. His family had accepted the Jewish religion and his wife was a Jewish princess. But he was still a foreigner to the Jews and he never won their friendship, even though he built the glorious Temple at Jerusalem for them.

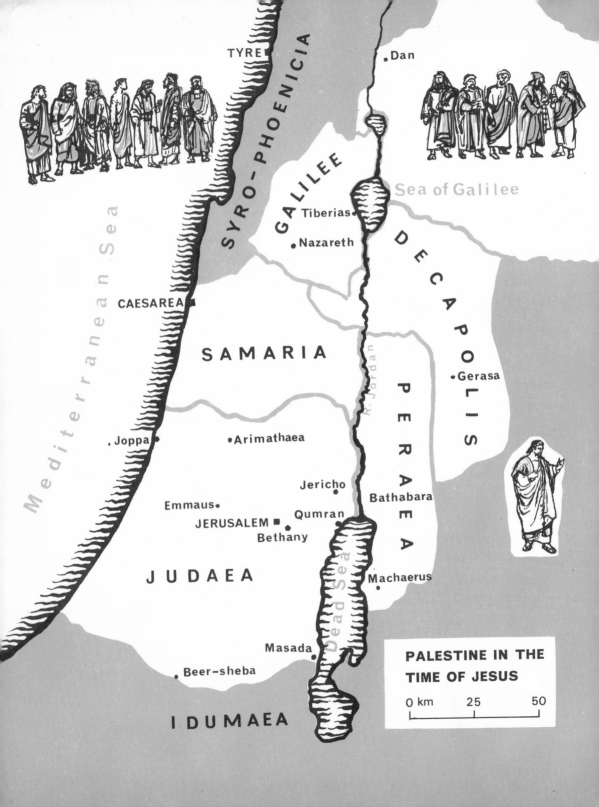

TYRE

Dan

SYRO–PHOENICIA

GALILEE

Sea of Galilee

Tiberias

Nazareth

DECAPOLIS

Mediterranean Sea

CAESAREA

SAMARIA

Gerasa

R. Jordan

PERAEA

Joppa

Arimathaea

Jericho

Bathabara

Emmaus

Qumran

JERUSALEM

Bethany

JUDAEA

Dead Sea

Machaerus

Masada

Beer-sheba

IDUMAEA

**PALESTINE IN THE
TIME OF JESUS**

0 km   25   50

Herod became ruler of the Jews by bloodshed and violence. Then the Romans made him King. He ruled over Judea from 37 B.C. to 4 B.C. We call him HEROD THE GREAT. Jesus was born towards the end of his long and cruel reign.

When Herod died he divided his kingdom among his three surviving sons. One of the younger sons, named HEROD ANTIPAS, was given Galilee and some land east of Jordan, where he ruled from 4 B.C. to A.D. 39. We shall hear more about him in the story of Jesus. The rest of the land east of Jordan was given to PHILIP, the other younger son.

The eldest son named ARCHELAUS was given the main part of Herod's kingdom—Judaea and Samaria, as well as Idumea. He should have become king like his father; but Archelaus was a foolish man and he caused the Jews to revolt again and again. The Roman Emperor was forced to dismiss him. In his place, Roman officials called PROCURATORS ruled over Judaea, Samaria and Idumea. One of them, named Pontius Pilate, ruled from 26 to 36 A.D. It was he who sentenced Jesus to death on the cross.

The Roman Procurator ruled from Caesarea—a fine city on the coast built by Herod the Great. He went to Jerusalem only when the city was packed with Jewish pilgrims at the time of the great feasts, when there was sure to be trouble. He was given about 3,000 troops to control the Jews and there were garrisons in all the main towns. They were not Roman soldiers but AUXILIARIES, men recruited from other lands to do military service for Rome. Four Roman legions were stationed in Syria, north of Palestine, where they could easily be called on if needed.

None of these soldiers were Jews for, as we saw, the Romans did not make Jews serve in their army. They were foreigners, pagans, and they carried the Roman Eagle as the symbol of all-conquering Rome. The Jews hated them.

Yet these troops gave Palestine peace and order, and some of them were friendly to the Jews. A Roman officer at Capernaum, for example, had even built a synagogue for the worship of the Jewish God.

ROMAN "EAGLES"

The standards of the Roman legions were like our flags and they were jealously guarded in battle. Made of gold or silver or bronze, they were decorated with the battle honours of the legion.

In early Roman times they were simply designs of animals. Later they became more decorated. But they were still called EAGLES and they were carried on long staffs by the EAGLE-BEARERS.

The Jews hated these standards. To them they were graven images, and so they broke the commandment of Moses. The Jews could not bear the Romans bringing them anywhere near their sacred places.

Pontius Pilate, the Roman Procurator, despised the Jews and often angered them. Once he ordered his troops to carry their standards, decorated with portraits of the Roman Emperor, into the Temple area of Jerusalem. The Jews rioted as soon as they saw them and Pilate was forced to remove them.

This tile, found near Jerusalem, bears the stamp of the Tenth Roman Legion: LEG—Legion; X-Tenth; FRE (tensis)—"of a narrow sea", "Straits of Sicily". The Tenth Legion was made up of warlike Gauls and Germans. It was this Legion which destroyed the monastery of the Essenes near the Dead Sea, and took part in the siege and capture of Jerusalem in A.D. 70.

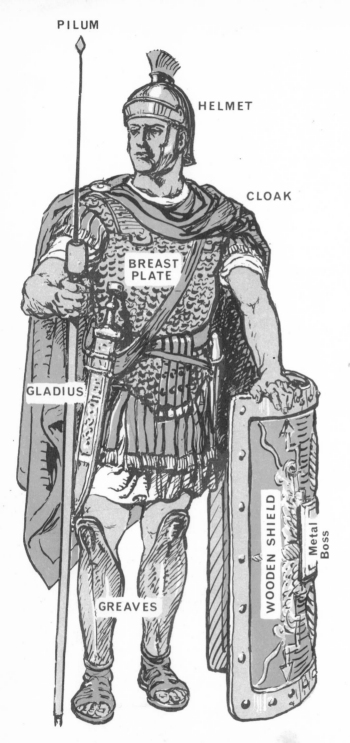

PILUM

HELMET

CLOAK

BREAST PLATE

GLADIUS

WOODEN SHIELD

Metal Boss

GREAVES

A ROMAN LEGIONARY

Helmet—made of metal, over a leather lining.

Breast-plate—made of metal, moulded as worn by Augustus (page 52), chain mail or over-lapping metal plates

Greaves—to protect the shins, made of metal—at this period worn only by centurions as a mark of distinction.

Shields—made of wood cover-ed with skin, with a frame-work and central plate of metal. Round and oval shields were also used.

Spear—made of light wood, 2 metres long, tipped with barbed iron to pierce an enemy's shield; called a "pilum".

Sword—the "gladius" was 50 cm long, broad and two-edged.

Light infantry used bow and arrows, a sling and a short javelin.

Horsemen carried lances and swords. They rode without stirrups.

Pilate had "auxiliaries" as his troops to rule Palestine, not Roman legionaries. There were five "cohorts" of foot soldiers (about 3,000 men) and one "wing" of mounted troops (about 500 men). But he could call on four legions of Roman troops (each of 5,500 men), stationed in Syria to the north of Palestine, if needed. The auxiliaries wore leggings and were only lightly armoured. Read Ephesians 6. 10-18 where Paul describes the armour of a Roman soldier.

A Roman legionary in battle. This is from a monument, made in the time of Emperor Trajan (98-117 A.D.), to commemorate the conquest of Dacia in Eastern Europe.

Jewish parties

The Jews were a proud race because they were God's chosen people. It was hateful to be ruled over by the pagan Romans and to have to pay tribute to their Emperor.

They had no need of an earthly ruler for God was their king. He had given them his Law by which to live. That was why they had no political parties, for they all accepted God's Law. They only differed in their attitude to it. That was why there were different religious groups.

Sadducees

The richest and most powerful group of Jews were called SADDU-CEES. Their name may mean either SONS OF ZADOK, the high priest of King Solomon, or RIGHTEOUS ONES. They were the priestly families of Jerusalem. Their leader, the High Priest, was recognised by the Romans as the leader of the Jewish people. They lived by the tithes and Temple Tax, paid by all Jews, and by the trading in the courts of the Temple. They believed strictly in the old Law of Moses, and they saw that the people paid their religious dues to the Temple, as the Law commanded.

The wealthy Sadducees were lordly in their ways and unpopular with the people. They were friendly to the Romans—just as they had been in earlier times to their Greek rulers. For if they were to keep their wealth and power they had to be on good terms with their overlords. Any trouble might give the Romans an excuse to take away their power. That was why they plotted to get rid of Jesus.

The Sadducees ruled through the SANHEDRIN or GREAT COUNCIL of the Jews. It was their highest court of law. It had 71 members many of whom were Sadducees, and the High Priest was chairman. The Sanhedrin had no authority in Galilee so that Jesus was safe as long as he stayed there. No wonder his disciples were afraid when he took the road to Jerusalem.

The Romans even allowed the Sanhedrin to pass sentence of death; but the Roman Procurator had to agree to it before the sentence could be carried out. That was why Jesus had to be taken before Pilate at his trial.

Scribes

Another party in the Sanhedrin were the SCRIBES. The word means WRITERS and in Old Testament times these were scholars who wrote out the sacred books of the Law. In time they became recognised as experts in the Law. They knew it, they studied it and they taught it, showing how it applied to daily life.

By the time of Jesus the Scribes were more important than the priests or Sadducees. The priests could only offer sacrifice in the Temple at Jerusalem. But Jews lived all over Palestine and all over the world. They worshipped God in their synagogues, where the Law was read and taught. Scribes were experts in the Law, not priests. If a decision was needed the Jew could only go to a Scribe, and his word was final. Scribes had become very powerful. They were respected for their learning—and sometimes feared.

The leading Scribes had their schools at Jerusalem. They were called DOCTORS OF THE LAW. Paul was proud of having been taught by the famous Scribe, Gamaliel. Such Scribes were addressed as RABBI—MY MASTER. Even more respectful was the title RABBONI—MY GREAT MASTER. Jesus was sometimes addressed in this way, for even a humble carpenter could be respected for his teaching.

The Scribes were learned men who loved the Law and lived by it. Yet Jesus condemned them and made them his enemies, too. They cared so much for the words of the Law of God that they had lost sight of its meaning, he said.

TEACHERS OF THE LAW

The special chair in the synagogue kept for the teacher of the Law—who might be a distinguished visitor—was called the "Moses' seat" (Matthew 23.2). This chair was found in the ruins of the synagogue at Chorazin, a town near Capernaum. It is made of black basalt.

Pharisees

About 200 years before the birth of Jesus the Jews were persecuted by Greek rulers. Greek customs and Greek gods were being forced upon them. How could they remain true to God and to his Law? The Sadducees thought that the best way was to keep on good terms with their pagan rulers. Then they might be more tolerant of Jewish customs, and Jewish religion. But other men thought that the only way was to separate themselves completely from the pagans and to live strictly by the Law of God. They were called SEPARATE ONES and that is the meaning of PHARISEES.

Once, these Separate Ones were attacked by their Greek rulers

This foundation-stone, with Greek inscription, was part of a synagogue built by Theodotus, a priest and ruler of a synagogue in the lower city of Jerusalem. It was in use before the destruction of the city in A.D. 70. There would have been many such synagogues in the city.

on the sabbath. They refused to fight on God's holy day and they died rather than defend themselves. In the time of Jesus the Pharisees would have nothing to do with the Romans. They certainly would not fight them. They did their best to ignore them, while the Sadducees were friendly with them.

The Pharisees lived by the written Law just as the Sadducees did. The difference was that they went further. They believed that God's law must be applied to every part of life. Thus they accepted new, unwritten laws and traditions handed down by the Scribes. They believed in angels and in spirits and in life after death – ideas which had come into Jewish religion since the time of Moses. The Sadducees would accept none of these beliefs. Many of the Pharisees were good and godly men. They helped to keep Jewish religion alive. Yet Jesus condemned them for being insincere, making a display of their religion to win the praise of men. The fussy rules they made for religion were heavy burdens upon the common folk, he said. So the Pharisees, too, became enemies of Jesus. Most of those who were members of the Sanhedrin gladly voted for his death.

Two of them did not. They were disciples of Jesus and they sought Pilate's permission to bury the body of their Master. Other Pharisees became members of the church of Jesus. One of them was the first great Christian missionary—Paul.

Zealots

The Sadducees kept on good terms with the Romans and the Pharisees avoided them. Others plotted against them. They were the ZEALOTS—an "underground movement" of fierce patriots who

36

could see no hope for their people until the Romans were driven out. Many of these conspiracies started in Galilee where Jesus lived. But the Zealots were not well organised. The Romans swiftly stamped out their revolts and crucified the ring-leaders, as well as their followers, as an example to others.

About 40 years after the earthly life of Jesus the Zealots raised the final revolt against Rome. They were led by fanatics called SICARII, or DAGGER-BEARERS, from the short dagger (in Latin— "sica") which they carried. The four years of bitter war ended with the terrible siege and capture of Jerusalem in A.D. 70. The Temple was utterly destroyed, as Jesus had foretold, and the Jews banished from Jerusalem. But by then the Jewish people had given a Saviour to the world.

One of the twelve apostles whom Jesus chose was a Zealot named Simon. Another, as we saw, was Matthew the tax-collector. Only love of Jesus could bring together one man who had fought against the Romans and another who had served them.

Essenes

Other groups of Jews showed their love for God in different ways. Some dedicated themselves to God by taking a vow for a certain time. These NAZIRITES, or DEDICATED ONES, vowed to keep certain old customs—not drinking wine, not cutting their hair, not eating

37

food forbidden by the Law, not going near the dead. Others went out into the wilderness for a certain time to be alone with God—as Jesus did before he began his ministry, and as Paul did, too.

Some Jews lived alone all their lives. These monks were called ESSENES—PIOUS ONES. Ancient writers described how they lived in the bleak and blazing desert at Engedi, near the Dead Sea—"with only palm trees for company," one of them wrote.

Nothing else was known about these monks till 1947. In that year a goatherd by chance found earthenware jars in a lonely cave up on the cliff by the Dead Sea. In them were leather scrolls wrapped in cloth. They are the famous DEAD SEA SCROLLS, a complete library

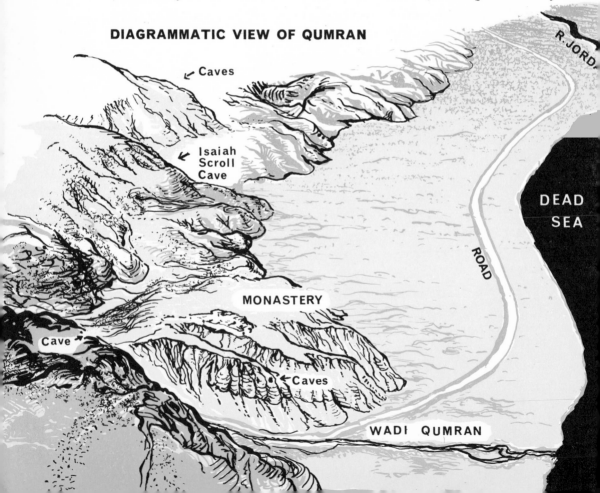

DIAGRAMMATIC VIEW OF QUMRAN

Caves

Isaiah Scroll Cave

Cave

Caves

MONASTERY

ROAD

WADI QUMRAN

R. JORD.

DEAD SEA

of ancient books. Scholars found among them many books of the Old Testament as well as other writings. They are very precious, for they are 1,000 years older than all our other manuscripts of the Old Testament.

But whose library was this? In 1951 scholars dug up the ancient ruins at the foot of the cliff by the Dead Sea called KHIRBET QUMRAN. They found the remains of the monastery where the Essenes had lived together. The library of books must have been theirs.

Why had they hidden them? The Essenes had lived in their monastery by the Dead Sea for over 100 years when the Zealots started the last war against Rome. In A.D. 68 the monastery was captured by Roman troops and the monks were killed or scattered. But they had time to hide their precious library safely in the caves where it was found almost 1900 years later.

From Qumran, the home of these Essenes, groups of monks went out to set up other lonely monasteries. They called themselves THE COMMUNITY, for they lived as brothers, sharing everything, eating communal meals and praying together at the appointed times. They worked hard to support themselves and fed only on the vegetables they grew. Each monk promised to be obedient to the rule of the Community, to remain unmarried and to own nothing of his own. Some Essenes lived quite alone. John the Baptist may have been one of these.

The Essenes were devoted to the Law of God which they kept strictly. Led by their priests, they had ceremonies of washing as symbols of their inner purity. Their simple white garment of linen cloth was also a symbol of the good life to which they were dedicated.

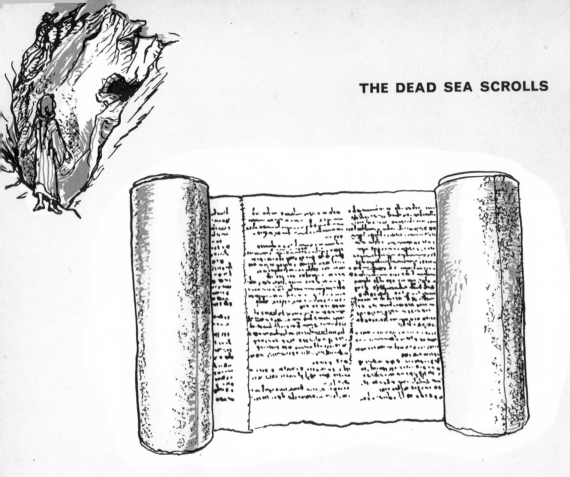

This is a scroll of the Book of Isaiah, found in 1947, hidden in a cave by the Essenes. It was made of parchment. Pieces, 26 cm wide, were stitched together to make a long roll of 7 m.

All Jewish books were scrolls, made of skin, papyrus or parchment. Every synagogue had its scrolls, kept in jars or chests in the "Ark". They were costly and precious and were, of course, regarded with great reverence, for they contained the sacred word of God. For reading aloud the roll was wound round a stick. This was held in the right hand and, as it was read, the scroll was wound round another stick in the left hand.

One Gospel tells how Jesus read in the synagogue service from the scroll of Isaiah (Luke 4.17-18). He read from Isaiah 61.1-2. The scroll opposite is open at Isaiah 40. But this scroll was being used in the time of Jesus and it must be very like the one from which he read.

The Dead Sea Scrolls were found in these earthenware jars, wrapped in cloth. The hot, dry atmosphere of the Dead Sea region had preserved them for 1900 years.

Some of the Qumran caves

The hope of a Saviour

All these were special groups among the Jewish people in the time of Jesus. What about the common people?

Those who lived in the towns, the BELLADEEN, had few worries. They were mostly well-to-do merchants and tradesmen, craftsmen and scribes. They wore fine clothes and lived in comfort.

Out in the desert were the BEDOUIN, just as there are today. They were nomads or wanderers, living by their flocks and herds, moving from one oasis to another for pasture and water.

Most of the Jews were FELLAHIN—workers on the land. They lived hard, simple lives—growing crops where they could, caring for their sheep, or earning a living as potters, carpenters or weavers. Their food was frugal, their dress was simple, their one-room houses were made of mud. They lived in villages in the countryside and seldom went to a town, except as pilgrims to Jerusalem.

Jesus, the carpenter of Nazareth, was one of these peasants. Life for them was hard. Many had to work for employers, when there was work to be had, and wages were not high. Some were little better than slaves. The burden of paying taxes twice over hit them hardest of all. What hope was there for better times?

The Jews had suffered all through their long history. More and more they longed for deliverance, for the kingdom of God to be set up among them. More and more they realised that their only hope was in God himself.

In the Old Testament we can read how prophets, men inspired by God, spoke of a hope for the future. God would send his ANOINTED ONE to his people. The Hebrew word for this Saviour was MESSIAH and the Greek word was CHRISTOS. From it we get our word

CHRIST. God's Anointed One would establish his kingdom on earth—a kingdom of peace and righteousness.

As things grew worse for the Jews this hope of a Saviour grew stronger. But it changed, too. People longed for a Christ who would save them from the worry over daily bread, giving them plenty for poverty. They longed for a Christ who would appear suddenly from heaven with great portents and signs and wonders, so that all men would bow down to him. They longed for a warrior Christ who would devour their enemies like a lion devouring its prey, setting them up in power and glory.

When the Saviour was born his mother named him JESUS—GOD SAVES. When his little band of followers recognised him as the Christ he was glad. But he was not the kind of Christ the people expected or wanted. Their leaders plotted against him and they had him executed. They thought that was the end of him. But it was really only the beginning.

TOWNSFOLK—BELADEEN
(Townsfolk)

In the towns lived merchants, shopkeepers, craftsmen, scribes, priests and government officials. Well-to-do merchants and important government officers could afford fine silk, imported from the Far East. Some of them wore a turban, closely wound around their heads. It had fringed ends, and it had been common head-dress, among wealthier Jews, for many centuries. Others even adopted the hat and coat worn by the Persians. The Jews had become familiar with this dress when their country had been part of the Persian Empire

DESERT-DWELLERS—BEDOUIN
(Desert-dwellers)

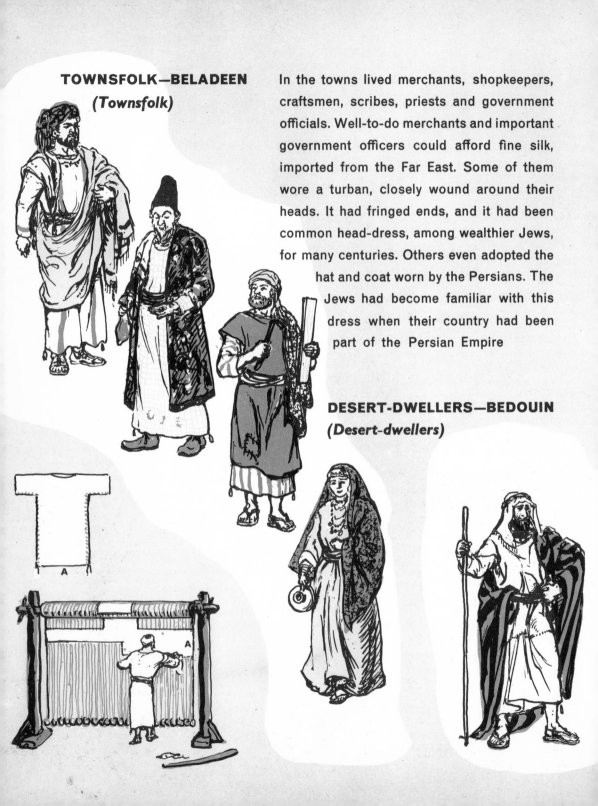

A

VILLAGERS—FELLAHEEN

Village people were much poorer than townsfolk. Their tunics were made of linen, and sometimes had no sleeves. A man tucked his tunic up into a belt when he started work. This was called "girding the loins" (Luke 12.35). The cloak of the villager was made of thick goat's hair or camel hair. It made a fine blanket for the cold nights. Over their heads the villagers wore a simple square headcloth. This protected the head and neck from the heat of the sun when they were working out in the open.

Nomads who wandered in the desert wore simple dress, made from the wool and hair of their flocks. Their cloaks, like those of the villagers, would have been black with brown or white stripes. Their headdress was probably like that of Arabs today—a fringed kerchief, or cloth, held in place with a ring made of goat's-hair. Like villagers and towns-folk, they used their girdle, or belt, as "pockets", tucking their money and food into it. Like the less well-off Jews, they wore sandals on their feet. These were quite simple and made at home from leather, with leather thongs to hold them to the feet (Mark 1.7).

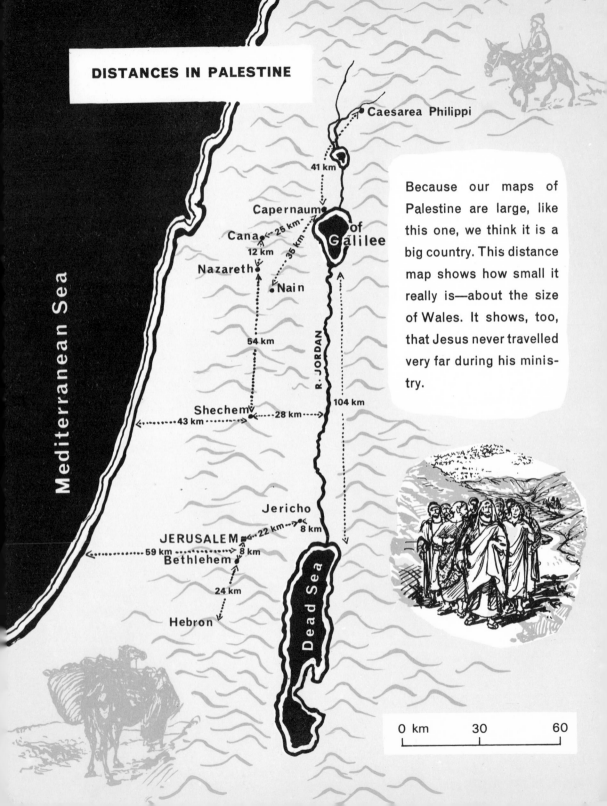

DISTANCES IN PALESTINE

Caesarea Philippi

41 km

Capernaum

Cana 25 km

12 km 35 km

Nazareth

Nain

of Galilee

R. JORDAN

54 km

Shechem 28 km

43 km

104 km

Mediterranean Sea

Jericho

JERUSALEM 22 km 8 km

59 km 8 km

Bethlehem

24 km

Hebron

Dead Sea

Because our maps of Palestine are large, like this one, we think it is a big country. This distance map shows how small it really is—about the size of Wales. It shows, too, that Jesus never travelled very far during his ministry.

0 km   30   60

To model

Make a relief map of the land of Jesus to show the four main divisions of Palestine. You can make it with alabastine or plasticene or papier mâché. Then you can colour it with green for low land, yellow for higher ground, and light and dark brown for hills and mountains. Show on your relief map the place names that you think are important.

To research

Choose the part of Palestine that interests you most and find out all you can about it. It might be the Plain of Esdraelon, or the River Jordan, or the hill country. Use reference books to help you in writing an account of it, with maps and illustrations. You will want to find out about the geography, the climate, the people, their work and customs and dress.

If you do this in groups, each group choosing a different part, you can make a class wall-chart of the land of Jesus.
Do not choose Galilee or Jerusalem as we shall come to them later.

To find out

Today the Jews in Palestine are working hard to restore their land, to reclaim the desert, and to develop the natural resources of their country. For example, they are using the waters of the Jordan to irrigate the land, setting up communities in the wilderness and extracting chemicals from the Dead Sea. Find out all you can about this exciting story. Reference books will help you. Newspapers often have stories of what the Jews are doing in Israel. You can also write to the Israeli Embassy in London for information.

Questions to answer

How did the land of Jesus come to be called "Palestine"?

What other names are there for this country?

Why was Palestine an important country when it was so small?

What other names does the Bible use for the Sea of Galilee?

Why can no one sink in the Dead Sea?

What were the differences in religion between the Jews and the Romans?

Why did the Jews hate the Romans so much?

What taxes did the Jews pay to their own country?

What taxes did the Jews pay to the Romans?

How did the Romans collect taxes?

Why did the Jews despise tax-collectors?

Who were the "Sadducees"?

What was the "Sanhedrin"?

Who were the "Scribes"?

Why did Jesus condemn the Pharisees?

Who were the "Zealots"?

Who were the "Essenes"?

What are the "Dead Sea Scrolls"? Why are they so important?

What were the three main groups of common folk among the Jews?

What hope did they have for the future?

To imagine

Imagine you were a young Roman soldier stationed in Palestine. Write a letter to your parents in Rome describing the country, the Jewish people, and why it is so difficult to get on with them.

Stories to look up

Jesus and the Temple Tax	Matthew 17. 24-27.
Jesus and the Roman Tax	Mark 12. 13-17.
Matthew Levi, a tax-collector at Capernaum	Luke 5. 27-32.
Zacchaeus, chief tax-collector at Jericho	Luke 19. 1-11.
A Pharisee and a tax-collector at prayer	Luke 18. 9-14.
Jesus and a Roman officer	Luke 7. 1-10.
Gamaliel, a Doctor of the Law	Acts 5. 17-40.
A Pharisee who came to Jesus by night	John 3. 1-8.
Two Pharisees who were disciples of Jesus	John 19. 38-42.
Jesus foretells the fall of Jerusalem	Luke 19. 41-44.

To act

Choose one of the stories above to act, using your own words. Others you can read together from the Bible, in dramatic reading, as if they were plays.

To draw

Choose one of the "Stories to look up" and draw it in a series of pictures as a strip cartoon.

To discuss

Why do you think some Jews went to live out in the wilderness as Essenes, leaving their cities and homes and friends? Why do you think people become monks and nuns? How do they serve God?

A wall-frieze to design

All the class can help to make a wall-frieze of Palestine in the time of Jesus. It will include all the different kinds of people, in their correct dress, with short accounts of their work. You can make town scenes and country scenes and design backgrounds for them, or special scenes of tax-collectors, fishermen, shepherds etc.

JEWISH CLASSES

Priest

Levite

Pharisee

Scribe

Tax-collector

THE ROMAN EMPEROR AUGUSTUS

Jesus was born during the reign of the Emperor Augustus. He ruled from 31 B.C. to A.D. 14., and Jesus was born about 5 B.C. Augustus ordered the census to be taken which took Mary and Joseph to Bethlehem. Read Luke 2.1.

Nazareth

B.C. and A.D.

We believe that the birth of Jesus was the most important event in all the history of the world. That is why it divides history into two parts. The first part is B.C.—everything that happened BEFORE CHRIST. The second part is A.D., letters which stand for ANNO DOMINI. These are words in the Latin language of the Romans which mean IN THE YEAR OF THE LORD.

Because of this division we naturally think that Jesus was born exactly between 1 B.C. and A.D. 1. But the man who worked out this dating made some mistakes. He was a monk named Dionysius Exiguus who lived at Rome about A.D. 533. In his day dates were worked out from the founding of the city of Rome in 753 B.C. Thus, he had to work out the beginning of the Christian era from the Roman Calendar. He did his work well. But it seems that he left out four years when the Roman Emperor, who decided to call himself Augustus, ruled under his own name. Also it seems that he forgot the year 0! Thus the new Christian Calendar was about five years wrong. But it was used more and more so that today we take it for granted.

This means that Jesus was in fact born about 5 B.C. We know this from the Gospels of Matthew and Luke. Both tell us that Jesus was born in the reign of King Herod the Great, which lasted from 37 B.C. to 4 B.C. Towards the end of his life Herod became mad with suspicion of plots against him. He even killed the wife he loved

53

best of all, as well as many of his sons. It would be quite like him to kill all the children of Bethlehem because Wise Men from the East believed that a new king had been born there.

Christmas

We keep December 25 as the festival of the birth of Jesus. But the Gospels do not tell us at what time of the year Jesus was born. Naturally Christians wanted to celebrate his birthday. It was in Rome, about A.D. 325, that they began to keep December 25 as the festival of Jesus' birth. It came to be called CHRIST MASS—the special Mass in honour of the birth of the Christ.

Why did they choose this day? It was mainly because December 25 was already a great, mid-winter pagan festival of the sun—the day when the sun was re-born at the winter solstice. Many people worshipped the sun in the ancient world. It was natural to think of Jesus as being the great Sun-God. "Sun of Righteousness" is one of the Bible terms for the Christ (Malachi 4.2). Besides, this would help pagans who became Christians. They could still keep their feast, but with a new and Christian meaning. Giving presents at this time was an old custom of the pagan Romans. Now Christians gave presents to each other in gratitude for the great gift of God—his son Jesus.

In the East Christmas is kept by some Christians on January 9 and by others on January 19. These differences do not matter. The important thing is to have a special day in the year when we remember the birth of Jesus and praise God for it. Christians call this the INCARNATION—from Latin words meaning IN THE FLESH. For we believe that in Jesus God became man.

54

Stories of the birth of Jesus

The first followers of Jesus knew nothing about how he was born or how he grew up. They knew a wonderful man whom they believed was the long-promised Saviour—the Messiah or the Christ. The very first Gospel was written by Mark. He had been the secretary of Peter, the apostle of Jesus. Peter had never said anything about the early years of Jesus. So Mark tells us nothing about the birth or boyhood of Jesus. He starts his Gospel when Jesus was a man and began to preach the coming of God's kingdom.

As time went on, Christians wanted to know everything about Jesus—how he was born, how he grew up, how he lived, how he taught, how he died and rose again. More Gospels were written to tell Christians everything that was remembered about Jesus. That is why the Gospels of Luke and Matthew tell us how Jesus was born.

Many Christians felt that the Saviour sent by God must have been born in a wonderful way and must have been able to do wonderful things as a boy. All sorts of stories grew up about Jesus the boy, and even more Gospels were made up. But these stories were really imaginary. They were just fanciful legends and Christians did not accept them.

All that we know about how Jesus was born and how he grew up is told in the Gospels of Luke and Matthew. Both of them tell us that Jesus was born in a wonderful way. But their stories are different from each other. We are going to follow the story told by Doctor Luke. We will keep the story in Matthew's Gospel separate.

Mary of Nazareth

In the little town of Nazareth there lived a carpenter named Joseph. It was a fine Jewish name and Joseph was a good Jew, following the faith of his fathers. He came from Bethlehem, the city of King David, and he could trace his descent back to David.

Nazareth was an unimportant place, tucked away in the hills, 24 km from the Sea of Galilee. There Joseph lived a quiet, godly life, working at his bench. In time he became engaged to a girl named Mary. The Jewish name MYRIAM meant BELOVED OF GOD. In Greek and Latin it became MARIA meaning THE LADY, and some Christians still call the mother of Jesus OUR LADY — in French NOTRE DAME and in Italian MADONNA.

Among the Jews marriages were arranged by the parents. The young couple were engaged for a year and then came the week of joyful wedding festivities. But this year of betrothal was as sacred as marriage itself. If, for example, the young man were to die during the year of engagement the bride would be regarded as a widow. It was also the custom among the Jews to marry young. This custom is still common in the hot lands of the East, for people grow up much earlier there. Mary would have been about fourteen years old when she became engaged to Joseph.

Their wedding would be planned for the autumn when the harvest was gathered in and the country folk could make merry after their hard toil. For everyone was invited—relatives, friends and the townsfolk of Nazareth. But it was during the year of betrothal that Mary had a vision of the "angel" or "messenger" of God. He told her that she was to become the mother of the long-awaited Saviour. She was to name him JESUS—the Greek form of the Hebrew name

JOSHUA which means GOD SAVES. We call this announcement to Mary the ANNUNCIATION, and artists have painted many beautiful pictures of it.

Mary was a devout girl, willing to do whatever God wanted. After the Annunciation she went to stay with her kinswoman, Elizabeth, who lived 128 km away in the hills near Jerusalem. There must have been a very close friendship between them and Mary wanted to share her secret with Elizabeth. She too was awaiting the birth of her baby, the future John the Baptist, and together they sang praises to God. Then Mary returned to Nazareth to await the birth of her child.

INNS

The inn or KHAN at Bethlehem where Mary had her baby may have been an ordinary house whose owners put up travellers for the night. Out on the open road a Khan was not much more than a shelter for the night. It would be made round a well and often on rock. A rough stone wall was built in a square with a covering of wood to make a courtyard. Today these inns are called CARAVANSERAIS—resting places for caravans.

A House Inn

An Inn on the road

An inn was not like a hotel. Travellers brought their own food and mattresses. They slept where they could. What the inn provided was shelter from the weather and from robbers, a place to sleep, and water.

One or two rooms were available. They were costly and only wealthy travellers could afford them. Read a story about an inn in Luke 10.25-37.

Bethlehem

It was at this time that the Roman Emperor, Augustus, ordered a census to be taken. This counting of the people was made by the Romans every 14 years so that they could tax the people. Everyone knew this and the census often caused a revolt. The rule was that everyone had to go back to the place where he came from to be enrolled, and this made the census even more troublesome. Joseph had to go back to Bethlehem, 136 km south. He took Mary with him, riding on the donkey. This meant that he accepted her as his wife.

BETHLEHEM means HOUSE OF BREAD, for the land around it grew good corn. It lay in the hills, five miles south of Jerusalem. It was an ancient, walled town with narrow streets and square, flat-roofed houses. It was crowded with people who had come back for the census. The little inn was packed out with travellers, some of them putting up for the night before continuing on the caravan

The Inner Courtyard

route south towards Egypt. Joseph found a shelter for Mary in a cave under the inn, used as a stable. There her child was born. As the custom was, the baby was washed, rubbed in salt to harden his skin, wrapped in swaddling clothes to make his limbs grow straight, and laid in fresh straw in the manger. There he would be warm and safe from the animals.

Doctor Luke's story goes on to tell how the messenger of God appeared to shepherds out on the hills, guarding their flocks from jackals and wolves; and how they came with gifts for the new-born child. In December it is very cold around Bethlehem. The animals are taken in from the frosty hills and kept safe indoors. So Luke's story suggests that Jesus was not born in December. Perhaps his birth was in early autumn.

A MANGER

It was a common custom for a mother to lay her baby in the manger during the day. It was safe and warm in the clean straw.

This ancient stone manger was found at Bethlehem. It shows how a baby would be laid in it, wrapped in swaddling bands.

This manger was found at Megiddo, a city of King Solomon. It was made of a hollowed-out stone, about 75 cm long. It was placed between two posts to which the horses of Solomon's chariots were hitched.

It was common in Palestine to use a cave as a stable. The manger would be cut out of the rock.

Every peasant house had a manger indoors, for the animals were brought in at night and tethered to it. The indoor manger was made of small stones joined together with mortar.

The baby was wrapped up like a Red Indian "papoose". It was placed diagonally on a square cloth which was folded round it. Then "swaddling clothes", strips of linen, were wrapped round it like bandages. Its hands were fastened to its sides so that it could not move. Swaddling a baby was believed to help its limbs grow straight. If a mother went out, she could carry her swaddled baby easily on her back. At night it slept in a cradle made of wood held up by two forked sticks.

The dedication of Jesus

The Jews loved children. It was almost a disgrace not to marry, and even worse to be married and not have children. The birth of a child was a great joy and it was celebrated with ancient customs, especially if it was a boy child.

A baby boy had to be circumcised on the eighth day. This made him one of the people of God. At this ceremony he was given his name. To the Jews, as to most ancient peoples, names were very important. The name of a person was part of him. Not only did it show what he would become; it also helped to influence his future. And since the Jews had no surnames it was even more important. A man was known simply as "the son of" his father.

Mary named her child as the messenger of God had told her. His name was JESUS which, in the language of the Jews, would be YESHUA. And since Joseph married Mary he was known, when he grew up, as YESHUA bar JOSEPH—Jesus son of Joseph.

The greatest joy of all to a Jewish family was when the first child to be born was a boy. He was called the BEKOR or FIRST-BORN. There was a very special ceremony for him. The Jews believed that the first-born of every living creature belonged to God, just as the first-fruits of the land belonged to him. So the child Jesus was HOLY or SET APART to God. He had to be offered to God in the ceremony of DEDICATION. If he was not going to belong to God as a priest he must be "bought back" by his parents.

Mary and Joseph had to pass through Jerusalem on their way back to Nazareth, so that it was very convenient for them to dedicate Jesus in the Temple. At the ceremony they had to sacrifice two turtle-doves or two pigeons. They also had to give five shekels

to the Temple treasury. This would be about £10 in English money—
a large sum for a humble carpenter.

    Doctor Luke's story of the birth of Jesus ends with his dedication
in the Temple. He tells how a devout old man named Simeon saw
in baby Jesus the promised Christ; and how Anna, a prophetess in
the Temple, joined him in praising God. Then Joseph took Mary
and the child back home to Nazareth and there Jesus grew up.

The story of the birth of Jesus in the Gospel of Matthew

The Gospel of Matthew was written specially for Jews. It was to show how all the prophecies of the Old Testament had come true in Jesus. Many of them, it says, were fulfilled in the birth of Jesus.

When Mary told Joseph of the child in her womb he was troubled. He knew that there would be gossip and disgrace for Mary if it became known. His first thought was to end his engagement to her. But he would do it quietly so that there would be no public disgrace for her. Then God spoke to him in a dream—for in those days dreams were believed to be messages from the gods. He was not to be ashamed of making Mary his wife, for the child within her was the gift of God. He would be known as IMMANUEL—GOD WITH US, the promised Saviour.

Then Joseph took Mary into his home, so making her his wife. When the time came to go to Bethlehem for the census he took her with him. There Jesus was born.

Wise men, guided by a star, came from the East to worship the new-born king. They went straight to the court of King Herod, seeking the child. There they learnt that the prophet had said the Christ would be born at Bethlehem, and they made their way there.

We are not told how many they were. Later tradition says that there were three—GASPAR ("White"), MELCHIOR ("Light") and BALTHASAR ("Lord of the Treasury"). Other stories say that one was young, one middle-aged, and the third an old man; and that one was white-skinned, another black-skinned, and the third yellow-skinned.

These men were MAGI—men who studied the stars, seeking

wisdom and knowledge from them. Still today there are people who believe in "astrology"—seeking to know the future from the positions of the stars. In those days there were "priests of the stars" in far-away Persia. They believed that the stars would foretell a heaven-sent deliverer.

The star they saw may have been a comet or even a new star. Some think that the bright light was due to the planets Jupiter and Saturn, in the constellation of Pisces, coming close to each other.

The Magi followed the star on their camels along the caravan route to the West. It was called the INCENSE ROAD; for along it travelled merchants with costly frankincense and myrrh to exchange for gold. These were the richest gifts they could offer to the child. Christians remember their coming to Jesus in the festival of the EPIPHANY—the MANIFESTATION or SHOWING of Jesus to Gentiles from afar.

Joseph feared the wrath of mad King Herod. He took Mary and the child down to Egypt, 240 km south. There they were safe when Herod slew all the young children of Bethlehem. In Egypt 9 km north of Cairo, lies the village of Mataria where they were said to have stayed, and where the little church is dedicated to "The Holy Family Exiled in Egypt".

Joseph returned from Egypt when he heard of Herod's death. But his son Archelaus ruled over Judaea and he was as cruel as his father. There was widespread revolt and bloodshed. Joseph avoided Judaea, travelling northwards along the coastal plain. He settled at Nazareth, a little town in the hills of Galilee, where there was peace and safety for his family.

GOLD

A Roman gold coin called an "aureus". This one was minted in the reign of the Emperor Claudius (A.D. 41-54).

Gold was used as a precious metal in Palestine from very early times. It was imported from the East. It was used for money by weight. In the time of Jesus there were gold coins (see Matthew 10.9).

Because gold was precious only great men could possess it. It was a symbol of a king.

FRANKINCENSE

The Boswellia tree from which comes frankincense

Incense was a white, scented gum which came from South-West Arabia, East Africa and India. It came from a tree called Boswellia. It was brought to Palestine by camel caravans from Arabia—the land of the Queen of Sheba. Incense was costly and precious. It was used in making holy oil for anointing. It was also burnt on the altars in the Temple at Jerusalem. Perfumes were also made from it.

Frankincense was a symbol of worship and therefore of holiness.

Read Luke 1.10.

MYRRH

Myrrh comes from a shrub called Commiflora

Myrrh came from another thorny bush, called Commiflora, which grew in Arabia and East Africa. It was an oily, yellow gum with a very sweet scent.

Myrrh was used by women especially for perfumes and cosmetics. It was also used for anointing the dead.

Myrrh was a symbol of suffering and of death. Read Matthew 2.11 and John 19.39.

The home at Nazareth

Joseph, the carpenter of Nazareth, was a humble workman — one of the fellaheen. His house was made of mud and straw, with wooden beams. It was white-washed and it had an outside staircase leading up to the flat roof. He worked at his trade in the "Street of the Carpenters". The advertisement over his shop may have read MY YOKES ARE EASY, MY BURDENS LIGHT, a saying which Jesus used when he called men to him. Our old English Bible says that Joseph was a "carpenter". The Greek word ("tekton") means WORKER IN WOOD. Since wood was used in so many ways— building houses, laying roofs, making furniture and farm implements—the wood-worker was much more than a carpenter. He was really a BUILDER.

Joseph had a large family to provide for. Besides Jesus there were four other boys—James, Joses, Jude and Simeon. There were also at least two girls. Joseph had to work hard to feed and to clothe them all, as well as to pay his taxes both to the Romans and to his own people. His taxes had to be paid in money, but he was often paid in kind—in corn or wine or oil, for example. Mary did her own spinning and weaving to make clothes, as far as she could. People wore a cotton undergarment, tunics and cloaks and sandals on their feet. Men wore their headdress and women wore veils. Often Mary had to patch the children's torn clothes.

The family lived on home-made bread, fish from the Sea of Galilee, different kinds of fruit, eggs and milk. One of the best meals was the evening stew that Mary made. Sparrows were used for meat. The lamb at the annual Passover Feast was a very special dish—and a very great luxury for a peasant home at Nazareth.

The house was all one room. It had a raised platform at one end where the family slept at night. The animals were brought in at night and tethered below, by the manger. Joseph would own an ass, a goat and chickens and they helped to warm the room at night. Furniture was simple. There were earthenware pots for oil and water and grain; a special chest for clothes and family treasures; millstones for grinding corn; and the precious oil-lamp which was kept burning day and night in the shadowy, windowless house. Beds were simply mattresses, rolled up and stored in a special alcove during the day.

A PEASANT'S HOME

This was the kind of home in which Jesus grew up. You can see it is all one room, with a platform at one end. Look for beds; jars for corn, wine and oil; mats on the earthen floor; animals on the lower floor; the beams on which the roof of mud and branches was laid.

Make a model of a peasant's home like this.

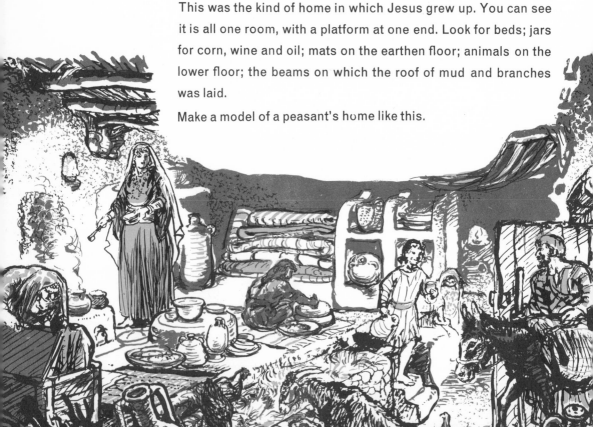

Wells in Palestine date from very ancient times. This is the well at Nazareth today, called "Mary's Well" ("Ain-sitt Miriam"). Until recently there was no other source of water in Nazareth or its surroundings, so this must have been the one used by Mary. As a boy Jesus would often have gone with his mother to the well, where the woman gossiped and the children played, as they still do, even though there is now tap water in the houses.

Jesus often helped his mother at her tasks—washing up; sweeping the earthen floor; grinding corn, heating the oven and making bread; filling, cleaning and lighting the lamp. He would go with her to the village well to draw water, Mary gracefully balancing the water-jar on her head.

69

Learning to know God

Jesus learnt his very first word from his mother. It was ABBA—
FATHER, the word for God that he loved best all his life. After the
evening meal Joseph took out the precious scroll of Scripture from
the family chest and read to his large family. He would tell them
stories of God's loving care for his chosen people, and of great
heroes of the Jewish faith.

Every Friday Jesus joined in the solemn preparation for the
sacred Sabbath; and on the Sabbath day he went with Joseph to
take part in the synagogue service. He would look forward to the
great festivals of the Jewish year—Passover and Pentecost and
Tabernacles, as well as the other feasts and fasts. For all of them
were observed in the home, and it was there that Jesus learnt to
know God.

Education was free for Jewish boys from the age of five to thirteen years. Jesus went with his friends to the synagogue school at
Nazareth. The people of Palestine spoke the Aramaic language, so
the boys had to learn Hebrew—the ancient language of their
people in which their Scriptures were written.

The boys sat on the ground, cross-legged, at school. They wrote
in the sand with their fingers, or sometimes with chalk on the flag-
stones. Their text-books were the Jewish Scriptures—our Old
Testament; in later times, in fact, school was called BETH HA-
SEFER—THE HOUSE OF THE BOOK. They learned to read the
sacred books, to write them out and to know them by heart. They
learnt the important passages by repeating them over and over
again. Every boy had to learn special texts which began and ended
with the first and last letters of his own name.

In the synagogue school the boys spent all their time learning their Bible, especially the sacred books of the Law of Moses. Even the alphabet was learnt from the Law. It was here that Jesus came to know and to love so well the Jewish Scriptures, for they spoke to him of the heavenly Father.

THE NAME OF JESUS

At the synagogue school at Nazareth Jesus learnt to read and to write. "Jesus" is the Greek form of his name. In the language of his people it was YESHUA. This is how he would have written it.

This writing was inscribed on a Jewish burial chamber. Yeshua was a popular name. We do not know who was the Yeshua buried here.

One of the stories in the Gospels mentions Jesus writing. Read John 8.6-8. Writing in sand was common. Boys often did this at school.

At play

Jewish children played their games in the open streets, on the flat roofs of their houses and out in the fields. Like children today they imitated grown-ups in their games. They played at mothers and fathers and at weddings and funerals, with processions and music and dancing.

Girls had dolls and model animals made of pottery or clay. Boys made pipes and whistles from reeds or played with a sling and

stones. Everyone played with pebbles. One game was called G A P—
throwing twelve pebbles in the air and seeing how many could be
caught on the back of the hand. Another was like hop-scotch.
Children played it on the flat roof of the house which was surrounded by a parapet so that no one could fall off. They drew
squares and numbered them and then threw pebbles into the
squares, one after another.

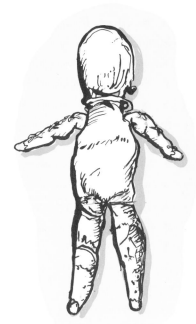

A Roman rag-doll of this time now in the British Museum. Jewish dolls would have had no features either, for the Commandments forbade the making of "graven images".

At work

Jesus had to work, too. The Jews had a saying – "If a man does not teach his son a trade he teaches him to be a robber." Fathers usually taught their own trade to their sons. Jesus learnt to be a woodworker. He would help Joseph to make yokes and ploughs for the farm, chests and stools and cradles for the home, doors and roof-beams and window-frames for new houses.

Jesus was well taught by Joseph and he became skilled in his craft. When Joseph died, Jesus took over his business. That was why everyone knew him as JESUS THE WOOD-WORKER when he was grown up. Rich and well-educated and important Jews, such as Scribes and Pharisees, looked down on humble craftsmen like wood-workers. They sneered at this wood-worker of Nazareth, setting himself up as a Rabbi.

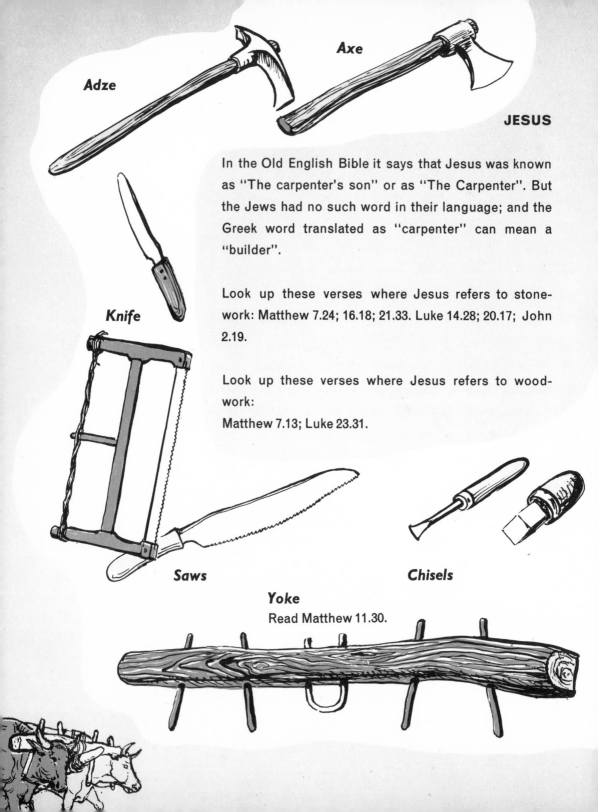

Adze

Axe

JESUS

In the Old English Bible it says that Jesus was known as "The carpenter's son" or as "The Carpenter". But the Jews had no such word in their language; and the Greek word translated as "carpenter" can mean a "builder".

Look up these verses where Jesus refers to stone-work: Matthew 7.24; 16.18; 21.33. Luke 14.28; 20.17; John 2.19.

Look up these verses where Jesus refers to wood-work:
Matthew 7.13; Luke 23.31.

Knife

Saws

Chisels

Yoke
Read Matthew 11.30.

Sycamore

Cedar

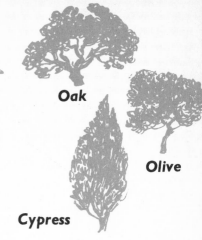

Oak

Olive

Cypress

THE WOOD-WORKER

The best wood was sycamore because it was worm-proof and hard. Cedar and oak were costly for they came from afar. Most commonly used were olive and cypress —or even trunks of old vines.

The wood-worker's tools were very like ours today: hammer and bronze nails, saw, knife, axe, hatchet, adze, plane, square and cramp. He also had the bow-drill which though very ancient, is still used today in the East.

Hammer

Roman Square

A Wood-worker of Palestine using a Bow-drill

NAZARETH

The city where Jesus grew up and worked. He would climb the hills in the distance.

Out of doors

Nazareth lay in the lap of the hills of Lower Galilee. Jesus had only to climb the hill to see far into the distance in all directions. To the north he could see snow-capped Mount Hermon. To the west was Mount Carmel. To the east lay the Jordan valley. To the south he looked over the great Roman road from Caesarea to Damascus, with its constant stream of travellers—soldiers, merchants, kings, camel caravans and well-laden asses, pilgrims and beggars.

Jesus loved to be out on the hills. In the wild flowers he saw God's beauty: in the birds of the air he saw God's loving care for every living creature. As he lay still on the grass he watched the bird returning to its nest, the eagle swooping on its prey, the fox creeping back to its hole.

Sometimes he went to the farms of his friends. He watched the workers scattering the seed, reaping and winnowing; he noticed how rich men stuffed their barns full to overflowing. He saw the mother hen tenderly sheltering her chicks under her wings. He helped the farmer to pull out an ox fallen into a pit.

Perhaps he loved best to be up on the hills with the shepherds, for he often spoke of them in his teaching. He knew the difference between the true shepherd and the hired man. The shepherd knew and loved each single one of his flock. just as they knew him and answered only to his voice. It was the hired man who fled when the ravenous wolf threatened the flock. He knew how the true shepherd, after counting his sheep at night and seeing them safely into the fold, would go back to search for even one lost lamb. And when he had brought it back, rejoicing, he would lie across the entrance to the fold all night. He himself was the door, keeping out wild beasts. So, by both night and day, the good shepherd guarded his flock, ready to defend them with his own life.

Jesus loved, too, to be with his friends the fishermen by the Sea of Galilee. He grew up with their sons. He helped them mend the torn nets, wash away the filth of the sea, and sort out the heaving catch. They learnt to know Jesus, too. When the day came that he called them they gladly left everything and followed him.

In the market-place and the streets of Nazareth Jesus saw all

kinds of people. He listened to the open-air lawcourt, learning how men's ways differed from God's ways. He saw hawk-eyed traders, cheating as they measured the corn; ragged beggars, crying out for alms; noisy news-mongers with tidings of happenings throughout the land; self-important Scribes and Rabbis; Pharisees praying at street corners, making a parade of their religion; tax-collectors piling up the coins at the customs-seat; merchants bargaining for a good sale, with dishonest oaths; blind men led by kindly friends. Even a boy could listen to what was being said. Jesus heard stories of travellers waylaid and robbed; of unjust judges and of dishonest stewards; of foolish sons who went off to waste their father's hard-earned money.

Jesus grew up like any other Jewish boy—at home, at school, at work and at play. When he was a man, teaching about God, he spoke to the people of things they knew and understood and made up stories about daily life. That is why we learn so much about his boyhood from his teaching.

The first visit to Jerusalem
Doctor Luke tells us the only story we have in the Bible of Jesus as a boy.

At the age of about thirteen years a Jewish boy left school. Still today a Jewish boy has his BAR MITZVAH, his coming of age, at this time. By this ceremony he becomes a SON OF THE LAW. Now he is regarded as an adult Jew. He is expected to recite the great prayer HEAR O ISRAEL three times a day; to fast on the appointed days; to keep the feasts; to attend the synagogue; and, of course, to go as a pilgrim to Jerusalem.

78

COOKING

Grain was bought in the market. A man often carried it home inside his cloak, above his waist-band (Luke 6.38). It was stored in a large jar in the house.

Flour was ground by the housewife for each meal. She had two mill-stones.

Grain was poured into the hole in the top one. The top mill-wheel was then turned by the handle made of wood. The flour collected around it. Sometimes two women did the grinding together (Luke 17.35). It was tiring work.

Cooking was done out-of-doors. The fire was made of charcoal or dried dung. A metal plate rested on stones over the fire. Flat bread or cakes made of flour and oil were cooked on the hot plate.

Cooking stove

The spice mill was made of wood or stone. Spices were ground in it till they powdered. The Jews were fond of spices with all their food. Find and read how Mary did her cooking—Luke 17.35; Matthew 6.30; Matthew 13.33.

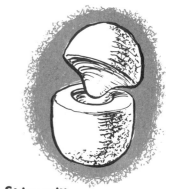

Spice mill

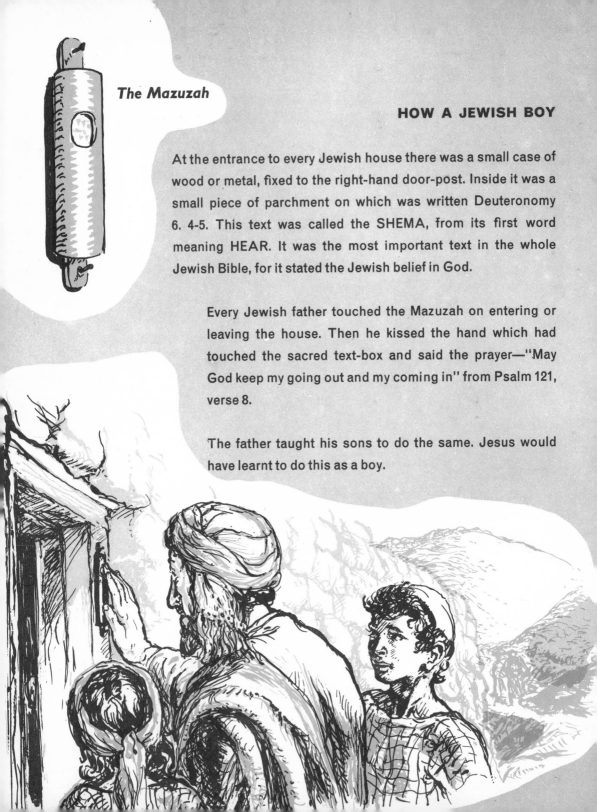

The Mazuzah

At the entrance to every Jewish house there was a small case of wood or metal, fixed to the right-hand door-post. Inside it was a small piece of parchment on which was written Deuteronomy 6. 4-5. This text was called the SHEMA, from its first word meaning HEAR. It was the most important text in the whole Jewish Bible, for it stated the Jewish belief in God.

Every Jewish father touched the Mazuzah on entering or leaving the house. Then he kissed the hand which had touched the sacred text-box and said the prayer—"May God keep my going out and my coming in" from Psalm 121, verse 8.

The father taught his sons to do the same. Jesus would have learnt to do this as a boy.

PRACTISED HIS RELIGION

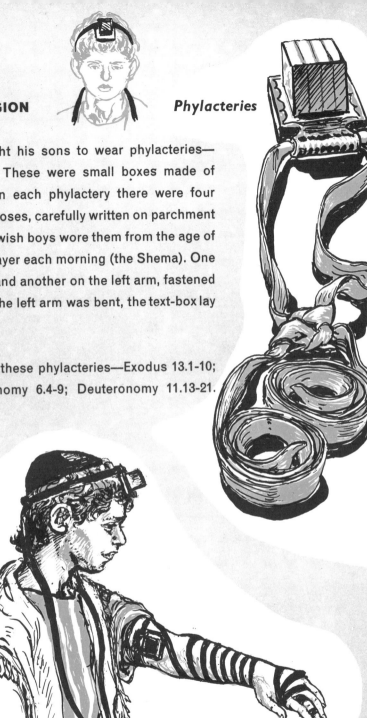

Phylacteries

A Jewish father also taught his sons to wear phylacteries—"guards" or "protectors". These were small boxes made of leather, cubes in shape. In each phylactery there were four passages from the Law of Moses, carefully written on parchment and bound with hair. All Jewish boys wore them from the age of 13 when saying the daily prayer each morning (the Shema). One was worn on the forehead and another on the left arm, fastened with leather straps. When the left arm was bent, the text-box lay directly over the heart.

Read the four passages in these phylacteries—Exodus 13.1-10; Exodus 13.11-16; Deuteronomy 6.4-9; Deuteronomy 11.13-21. Look up Matthew 23.5.

The Parchment in the phylactery box

When Jesus left school and came of age he was ready to make his first pilgrimage to Jerusalem. Joseph and Mary took him with them for the greatest feast of the year—the Passover, in the spring. There, with the other boys of his age, he would be examined by the Doctors of the Law.

The journey of 128 km to Jerusalem took three days. They travelled with friends and relatives from Nazareth in a caravan for safety and company, camping by night. Jesus must have been enthralled by all that he saw in Jerusalem, above all at the Temple of God, for on the way home Mary and Joseph found that he was missing. They had thought that he was with his friends, but he was nowhere to be found. Anxiously they hurried back to Jerusalem. There at last they found him. He was still with the Rabbis, seeking answers to questions that puzzled him. They were astonished by his knowledge and understanding of the Scriptures and by the questions which he asked. Mary spoke crossly to her son for being so thoughtless and giving his parents such a lot of worry. "But why were you searching for me?" Jesus said to her, "Didn't you realise that I would be in my Father's house?"

Luke's story shows us that already, even as a boy, Jesus was completely dedicated to God.

The silent years
Jesus went back home to Nazareth with Joseph and Mary. He was a good son, obedient and dutiful.

The next we hear of Jesus is when he left home at Nazareth to begin his work for God. He was then about thirty years old. We know nothing about him from the age of twelve to the age of thirty. We call these THE SILENT YEARS. What was Jesus doing during that time?

Some Jewish boys went on to study at Jerusalem after they left the local synagogue school. They were usually boys who were going to become Rabbis. At Jerusalem they were taught by the great Doctors of the Law. One of them was Paul who was proud of having been taught by the famous Rabbi Gamaliel. It was like going to a university. But it was very expensive. Paul came from a wealthy home. Jesus came from a village wood-worker's home. We can be certain that there was no money for Jesus to study at Jerusalem. But we can be sure that he went to Jerusalem each year for the Passover as a pilgrim.

What then was Jesus doing during the Silent Years?

When he began to preach at Nazareth the people said, "Why, this is Yeshua bar Joseph the wood-worker!" They knew him well enough. So we can be sure that Jesus was at Nazareth during those years. Joseph is not mentioned again when Jesus began to teach. He must have died when Jesus was a young man. Jesus had taken over Joseph's shop. He too had to work hard to provide for his widowed mother and her other six children. He did not leave home until they were old enough to care for Mary, and until the time had come for him to preach the kingdom of God.

These ancient Jewish oil lamps were found near Jerusalem. They are the kind of lamps used in the home of Jesus at Nazareth.

In the peasant's house, light came from an oil lamp. It was made of clay or earthenware—sometimes, in a rich man's house, of metal. It had a hole at one end to pour in the olive oil that it burnt. The wick, made of flax or hemp, was put in the other opening. Windows, if any, were small, to keep the house cool, so that the house was dim. The lamp was often kept burning all day. It was also useful for lighting fires.

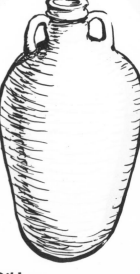

The olive oil for the lamp was stored in large jars, about three feet high.

Funnel

Oil Jars

**Lamp found
at Qumran**

Lamp Stands

The lamp burnt all night, too, for the Jews did not like the dark. The good wife made sure her lamp never went out at night (Proverbs 31.18).

Some houses had a niche in the wall for the lamp. Most of them used a stand—see Matthew 5.15. Many such lamp-stands have been found in Palestine, made of wood or clay or metal. Sometimes the lamp itself was part of the stand. Candlesticks were used, of course, for candles.

**Lamp holder
of the period**

**Roman hanging
lamp**

To read together

The story of the birth of Jesus in the Gospel of Luke:

The Annunciation	Luke 1. 26-56.
The Birth of Jesus	Luke 2. 1-7.
The Visit of the Shepherds	Luke 2. 8-20.
The Circumcision and Naming of Jesus	Luke 2. 21
The Dedication of Jesus	Luke 2. 22-40.
A story of the boy Jesus	Luke 2. 41-52.

Parts of these stories you can read dramatically, as if they were plays. Other parts can be spoken in a chorus by the whole class.

To write in your note-book

There are some important new words in this chapter for you to write and to explain in your note-book

Incarnation; Our Lady; Angel; Jesus; Annunciation; Dedication of the firstborn; Immanuel; Magi; Astrology; Epiphany: Abba; Bar Mitzvah.

To read together

The story of the birth of Jesus in the Gospel of Matthew:

Joseph's dream	Matthew 1. 18-25.
Wise Men from the East	Matthew 2. 1-12.
Flight to Egypt	Matthew 2. 13-18.
Settling at Nazareth	Matthew 2. 19-23.

Parts of these stories you can read as if they were plays choosing a reader for each character. Other parts can be spoken in chorus by the whole class.

To write out and remember

In the Gospel of Luke there are some wonderful hymns of praise:

The Song of Mary (Magnificat)	Luke 1. 46-55.
The Song of Zacharias (Benedictus)	Luke 1. 68-79.
The Song of the Angels	Luke 2. 14.
The Song of Simeon (Nunc Dimittis)	Luke 2. 29-32.

These are so fine that they are still used in church services today. You can read them through together in chorus. You can write them out in your very best writing—in "illuminated" writing, if you can. This will help you to remember them. They are fine passages to have stored away in your memory.

To look up

Here are important passages which Jesus had to learn at school:

Hear O Israel (Shema)	Deuteronomy 6. 4-9.
The Praise (Hallel)	Psalms 113 to 118.
The Commandments of Moses	Exodus 20. 1-17.

Read these passages as you have time. You can learn some of them by heart too—especially the Commandments of Moses.

To model

There are many things for you to make and model in this story of the boyhood of Jesus:

The kind of house he lived in; the furniture of the house; children's toys; an oil-lamp; mill-stones; a scroll of Scripture, with the Shema or the Commandments written on it; the wood-worker's tools; a sheepfold; the shepherd's implements.

Answers to be looked up

Find the answers to these questions about Jesus:

Did Jesus have any brothers and sisters? (Mark 6.3; Matthew 13.55-56).

What was a peasant house like? (Luke 11.5-7; Luke 15.8)

What was the first word Jesus learnt from his mother? (Mark 14.36)

Could Jesus read and write? (Luke 4.16-17; John 8.6)

What books did Jesus read? (Luke 4.16-17; Matthew 12.3-7;15. 7-9)

Was the family of Jesus rich or poor? (Mark 2.21; Luke 12.6)

What food did the family of Jesus eat? (Matthew 10.29; 7. 9-10)

What games would Jesus have played? (Luke 7.32)

What work did Jesus watch Mary doing? (Mark 2.21; Matthew 6.30; Matthew 13.33; Luke 17.35; Luke 15.8)

How would Jesus help at home? (Matthew 5.15; Matthew 23.25)

What trade did Jesus learn? (Matthew 13.54; Matthew 11.30)

Questions to be answered

What do we mean by the letters B.C. and A.D.?

How did December 25 come to be kept as Christmas Day?

What were the marriage customs of the Jews?

Why did the Romans order a census to be taken? How was it done?

What was special about a first-born son?

What kind of school did Jesus go to?

What games did children play?

What kind of work did Jesus do?

How did Jesus learn about God?

To imagine

Imagine you were a boy or girl at Nazareth when Jesus lived there. Write or tell an account of how you lived. You will need to describe your home, food, clothes, school, church, games, and the town itself.

To find in your hymnbook

Find hymns about the birth and boyhood of Jesus and read them together. Learn a new one to use in School Assembly.

A street in Nazareth, showing
a carpenter's shop and house,
with yard at back.

Galilee

John the Baptist

Doctor Luke tells us in his gospel that Jesus was about thirty years old when he left his home at Nazareth. It was the year A.D. 28. Why did Jesus start his work for God at that time? It was because John had begun to baptise by the river Jordan.

John the Baptist was the son of an old priest named Zacharias. His wife, Elizabeth, also came from a priestly family. They lived in the village of Ain Karem, 6 km or so west of Jerusalem. There John was born, about three months before the birth of Jesus, and there he grew up.

You will remember that Mary went to visit Elizabeth when she knew that she was to become the mother of Jesus; for Elizabeth was her kinswoman and her close friend. They must have gone on seeing each other as their sons grew up, especially at Jerusalem when they went there each year for the Passover Feast. Jesus and John were about the same age, as well as being related to each other. They would often have talked about God, and about the Saviour whom he would send to his people. Perhaps John realised, even when Jesus was still a boy, that he was the promised Messiah.

The name JOHN means GIFT OF GOD. His parents had dedicated him to God, like one of the Nazirites. As John grew up he knew that he had a special work to do for God. He should have been a priest at Jerusalem like his father. Instead, he went out to live a hard and lonely life in the wilderness between Jerusalem and the Dead Sea.

We cannot be sure that John became one of the monks called Essenes who lived out there in their monastery. They lived together, but John lived alone. They lived on the vegetables they grew. John lived on insects called locusts, like the desert wanderers, and on honey from the wild bees. They wore garments of white linen. John wore a rough cloak made from camel's hair, tied with a leather belt, like the poorest peasants.

A STATUE OF TIBERIUS, EMPEROR OF ROME

Doctor Luke tells us in his Gospel that it was in the 15th year of the reign of Tiberius that John the Baptist began to preach.

Tiberius reigned from A.D. 14-37. So this was the year A.D. 28.

The ministry of Jesus lasted from A.D. 28 to 30, during the reign of Tiberius.

The ministry of John

Suddenly, in the year A.D. 28, John left the wilderness and began to preach by the river Jordan; for now he was ready. He chose a fine place called BETHABARA—which means HOUSE OF THE FORD. The route along by the river Jordan was a main road for travelling Jews, and they forded the river just there. The news spread like wildfire. People flocked out from towns and villages to hear John. For 400 years there had been no prophet like him. Could John be the Christ whom everyone longed for so much?

John was harsh and stern in his preaching. He spoke of the anger of God with evil-doing, not of his love for evil-doers. He told the crowds to give up their evil ways, to come down in the water and to be washed of their sins. Time was short. The Messiah was coming. John was preparing the way.

Some people recognised who John was. For a long time the Jews had believed that the great prophet Elijah would come back to earth. He would be the herald of the Messiah. Didn't John look like him, dress like him, live like him? "Yes", John said, "I am like a herald, the slave who runs before a royal procession shouting, 'Clear the road! Make way for the king!'" John was fulfilling the prophecies of the herald of the Messiah.

Many people believed in John. They were sorry for their sins and they went down into the water to be baptised. Young men became his disciples. John taught them to pray, to fast and to baptise.

Then, one day, John saw his kinsman Jesus coming down into the water. He was glad, for it meant that Jesus recognised him as the herald. But John was humble, too, at baptising the Messiah.

Jesus had a wonderful experience of God as he stood there, in the river. He described it afterwards to his disciples in the very words of the prophecies. It had seemed to him that the heavens had opened and that the Spirit of God had come down upon him, like a dove gently settling on his shoulder. He had heard God's voice, in the words of Scripture, saying, "Thou art my Son." So the prophecies of the Messiah were fulfilled.

WINNOWING

When he was a man John the Baptist went to live in the wilderness, but he had been brought up in the country, at his parents' home in the hill country of Judaea. He knew all about the ways of agriculture. He must often have helped on the local farms as a boy, gathering, threshing and winnowing the corn.

John spoke of winnowing in his preaching. It was the method of separating the precious grain from the useless chaff. The wheat or barley was thrown into the air with a wooden fork, or even with forks and shovels, during the breeze of late afternoon. The grain fell on to the threshing floor where it was heaped to-

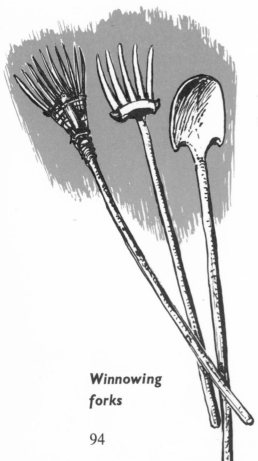

Winnowing forks

94

gether with wooden shovels and then stored in barns. The chaff, blown away by the breeze, was gathered up later for burning or for fodder. John's preaching was stern and fiery. He said God would separate men like that, the good from the bad.

Read about winnowing in Ruth 3.2; Isaiah 30.24; Psalm 1.4 and 35.5; Matthew 3.11-12.

Read the parable Jesus told about the rich and selfish man, whose barns were stuffed full, in Luke 12.16-21. What do you think Jesus meant by it?

Jesus told other parables about separating good from bad. You can read them in Matthew 13.24-30 and 47-50; Matthew 25. 31-46.

A man winnowing

Chaff

Grain

His Dress

John the Baptist wore "a raiment of camel's-hair". Still today Bedouin wanderers and shepherds wear an "abayeh" —an outer cloak or mantle made of hair from goat or camel. The hair is clipped from the neck, back and hump of the camel and woven into cloth on hand looms. The cloak lasts a lifetime. It protects the wearer against heat by day and cold by night, as well as rain and dust. It could be used as a carpet or as a tent.

John lived a hard and strict life. His garment may have been simple and short and worn without a tunic underneath.

IN THE WILDERNESS

His Food

John lived on wild honey and locusts. These grasshoppers are often mentioned in the Bible. In Bible times, and still today, an invasion of locusts can be a disaster, for they settle on crops and trees and devour everything.

But locusts can also be eaten for food. They are caught in the morning when they are numb with cold or their wings are wet from dew. Their bodies are boiled in salt water or roasted. Sometimes they are dried in the sun, and ground into powder for making cakes mixed with honey for sweetness. Here are some Bible references about locusts for you to look up: Psalm 78.46 and 105.34; Joel 1.4; Joel 2.25; Job 39.20; Joel 2.1-3.

His Company

There were no plants in the burning wilderness where John dwelt. Lizards, scorpions and vultures were the only living creatures in the wilderness—apart from vipers or poisonous snakes. When the pious Pharisees and Sadducees came to hear John he called them "a brood of vipers". Vipers stood for evil in the Bible (see Isaiah 30.6 and 59.5; Job 20.16). For evil men were like these repulsive snakes which were filled with poison.

The death of John

Now that John had prepared the way his work was done. Some of his disciples left him to follow Jesus and he knew that was how it should be. He did not have much longer. Already the Scribes and Pharisees were angry with him for his bitter words against them. The High Priest had sent messengers to examine him. For John's preaching and his popularity could be dangerous.

Herod Antipas, a crafty and suspicious ruler, thought so too. John baptised in his territory. First Herod sent spies and then he had John arrested. Herod knew that he was unpopular. John might turn people against him even more. He could cause trouble with the Romans, too. Yet Herod was superstitious and he feared John, for he knew that he was a holy man.

Herod shut John up in the fortress of Machaerus. It had been built by his father, Herod the Great, on a mountain peak east of the Dead Sea. It was a lonely, desolate place; John lay in a dungeon cut deep in the rock, where today desert nomads shelter their animals. He began to have doubts. Was Jesus really the Christ or not? When two of his disciples came to visit him he sent them to ask Jesus. They came back and told John how Jesus was making the Kingdom of God known in his words and in his deeds.

It was Herod's wife who had persuaded the king to imprison John. John had condemned Herod for marrying her unlawfully and she hated John for it. Now she tricked the king during a party into having John beheaded at the fortress.

Jesus said that there had never been a greater man than John, for he had been the herald of the Messiah.

The temptations of Jesus

After the wonderful experience at his baptism, Jesus went out into the wilderness to be alone with God. He had to think out his work. How would he do it? What kind of Messiah would he be? Later, he described to his disciples what happened there.

It seemed as if the devil said, "Turn these stones into bread. That will prove you are the Christ." It was a great temptation. Jesus knew just how hard life was for the peasants, trying to make a living, to feed their children, and to pay taxes twice over. They wanted a Christ who would give them all they needed, turning their poverty into plenty. But Jesus knew that was not God's way. That would not change people or set up God's kingdom of goodness and love. The Scripture said that men needed the word of God as well as bread—food for their souls as well as food for their bodies.

Then Jesus imagined himself to be on the highest pinnacle of the Temple at Jerusalem—on the portico at the south-east which jutted out 39 m above the deep valley of Kidron. "Throw yourself down," said the devil, "Doesn't the Scripture say that God will protect you?" That would please the people, too. They expected a Saviour who would come down on the clouds of heaven. But would miracles and wonders bring men to love God and to live together as one family in love and brotherhood?

The third temptation was the worst. "Do it my way," said the devil, "Then you could drive out the Romans and build up your kingdom." Many Jews longed for a warrior Messiah to defeat the Romans and set up God's kingdom. They would flock to Jesus if he proclaimed himself their leader. But Jesus knew that bloodshed and battle and destruction could not bring men to peace and to brotherhood. That was the way of the devil, not the way of God.

Jesus refused all these easy ways of winning the people to God. He would not give them food—or miracles—or power. He would show men the kingdom of peace and goodness and love in his own life, and he would gather others to share in it. This was the hard way. It would lead to unpopularity, to suffering, even to death. But one of the prophets had described a Messiah like that—one who would serve God faithfully in life and in death. That was the way Jesus would take.

It was hard for people to understand this kind of Messiah. It was hard even for Jesus' own disciples. They did not really understand —not till he had died and risen again.

Twelve apostles

Jesus needed helpers in his work. They would be the beginning of the kingdom. Then they could preach it to others.

DISCIPLES or FOLLOWERS gathered round Jesus. From them he chose twelve to be APOSTLES or MESSENGERS. Why should it be twelve? The Jews, the chosen people of God, had come from the twelve "Patriarchs" or "Heads of Tribes". The twelve apostles were to be the founders of the new people of God.

Eleven of the apostles were men from Galilee. Four of these were fishermen on the Sea of Galilee—the brothers Andrew and Simon Peter, and the brothers James and John. Matthew had been a tax-collector at Capernaum. Simon had been a Zealot. Bartholomew Nathaniel came from Cana and his friend Philip from Bethsaida. The other three Galileans were Thomas Didymus, Jude and James the Less—that is, "James the Younger".

The twelfth apostle was Judas Iscariot. ISCARIOT means MAN OF KERIOTH. Kerioth was a village in Judaea, so that Judas was the "odd man out"—the only one who did not come from Galilee. Some people think that "Iscariot" may come from the Greek word "Sikariotes" meaning "Dagger-bearer". This would mean that Judas was a fierce patriot who hated the Romans and fought against them. Judas was a clever man and he looked after the money for all the apostles.

Peter, James and John seem to have understood Jesus best of all. That was why he chose them out of the twelve to be with him always.

Simon Peter

THE TWELVE APOSTLES

Simon was the natural leader of the twelve apostles and one of three whom Jesus took everywhere with him. He was a fisherman from Bethsaida and lived at Capernaum. Jesus gave him a new name—Cephas or Peter which means Rock.

Peter was the natural leader of the early Christians.

He finally went to Rome where tradition says that he was crucified upside down. He died about A.D. 64 during the persecution by Nero.

His symbol is a pair of keys, for tradition said that he is the doorkeeper of heaven. This is based on the saying of Jesus in Matthew 16.16-20. His day is June 29.

Write a biography of Peter from: Luke 5. 1-11; Mark 3.16; Matthew 14. 22-33; Matthew 16.13-23; Matthew 17. 1-8; John 18. 1-11; Luke 22. 54-62; John 20. 1-10; John 21. 1-19; Acts 1. 15-26; Acts 2. 14-43; Acts 3. 1-11; Acts 4. 1-22; Acts 8. 14-24; Acts 9. 32-35 and 36-43; Acts 10. 1-48; Acts 12. 1-17.

Andrew

Andrew, Simon's brother, was also a fisherman. He had been a disciple of John the Baptist and, according to one story, brought Simon to Jesus (John 1. 35-40). He lived with his brother at Capernaum.

Andrew's day is November 30. Tradition said that he was a missionary in Greece and in Asia Minor, and that he was crucified upon a cross shaped like an X. Thus the St. Andrew's Cross became his symbol.

Read more about Andrew in: Mark 1. 16-18; John 1.40-42; John 6. 5-14; John 12. 22.

AND THEIR SYMBOLS (1)

James and his brother John were, with Simon Peter, the closest of the twelve to Jesus. They were sons of Zebedee, a well-to-do fisherman of Galilee. Their mother Salome stood by the cross of Jesus with his mother Mary. She may have been Mary's sister. James and John left their fishing business to follow Jesus.

James was the first of the apostles to be put to death. He was beheaded by Herod in A.D. 44 (Acts 12. 2).

James is remembered on July 25. His symbols are the staff and wallet of a pilgrim. You can read more about him in: Mark 1. 16-20; Mark 3. 17; Mark 10. 35-45; Mark 9. 2; Mark 14. 32-42.

James the Elder

John was a fisherman like his brother James. They were so alike, too, in character that Jesus nicknamed them "Sons of thunder" or "Sons of anger" (Mark 3. 17). With his brother and Simon Peter he was always close to Jesus (Mark 5. 37; Mark 9. 2; Mark 14. 33). It seems that John was the "beloved disciple" spoken of in John's Gospel. Read about him in John 13. 23; 19. 26-27; 20. 1-10; 21. 1-7.

Tradition says that John lived and taught at Ephesus in Asia Minor and died there in old age. Some think that his Gospel was written by John himself, others that it was written down by another John who had heard the memories of the apostle when he was an old man.

John is remembered on December 27. His symbols are a cup (or chalice) with a winged serpent. For legend said that a pagan priest dared John to drink a cup of poisoned wine. John made the sign of the cross over the chalice and the devil, in the shape of a snake, flew out of it. Then he drank the harmless wine.

John

James the less

THE TWELVE APOSTLES

The other apostle named James is called "The Less" or "The Younger" to distinguish him from James, the brother of John (Mark 15. 40). His mother and father and brothers were also followers of Jesus. His mother, another Mary, was with the mother of Jesus by the cross (Mark 15. 40-41; Mark 15. 47; Mark 16. 1).

James is remembered on May 1. He is said to have preached in Palestine and in Egypt and to have been crucified. His symbol is a saw for he is said to have been sawn to death.

Jude

Jude or Judas (not Iscariot) is mentioned in Luke 6. 16; John 14. 22; Acts 1. 13. He is said to have travelled to Persia as a missionary, and hence his symbol of a sail-boat with a cross-mast. Tradition also says that he died as a martyr in Persia. He is remembered on October 28.

Philip was a friend of Andrew and Peter and like them came from Bethsaida by the Sea of Galilee. He seems to have been a shy and simple man. You can read about him in John 1. 43-46; John 12. 20-23; John 14. 8-21; Acts 1. 12-14. It seems that Philip looked after the food for the band of apostles (John 6. 5-7). Hence his symbol—two loaves of bread. He is said to have preached in Asia Minor and to have died a martyr's death. May 1 is his day in the Christian year.

Philip

AND THEIR SYMBOLS (2)

Bartholomew's other name was Nathaniel. He was brought to Jesus by Philip and their names were always linked together. He came from Cana in Galilee. You can read about him in John 1. 45-51; John 21. 1-14. His symbols are a Bible and a flaying knife for he is said to have been flayed to death. He is remembered on August 24.

Bartholomew

Matthew, or Levi, was a tax-collector at Capernaum when Jesus called him (Luke 6. 27-32). The first Gospel was named after him because it contained a collection of sayings of Jesus made by him. He was said to have died a martyr in Ethiopia. His symbol, three money-bags, reminds us of his calling. September 21 is the day set aside to his memory in the Christian year.

Matthew

Thomas other name, Didymus, means "Twin". He was brave and loyal to Jesus (John 11. 8 and 16). But he was slow to believe that Jesus had risen from the dead till he saw him (John 20. 24-25 and 26-29). From him we get our saying "a doubting Thomas". Thomas is said to have preached in Syria, Persia and India. He was killed by a shower of arrows while he was praying. His symbol is a spear and a carpenter's square. He is remembered on December 21.

Thomas

Simon

THE TWELVE APOSTLES AND THEIR SYMBOLS (3)

Matthew, a Jew collecting taxes for the Romans, had been a traitor to his people. Simon was just the opposite—a fierce patriot. He had been one of the Zealots, men who fought against the Romans secretly to free their country. Read Luke 6. 15 and Acts 1. 13.

Tradition said that Simon died by crucifixion. His symbol is a fish on a hook, for he came from Galilee and may have been a fisherman. He is remembered, with Jude, on October 28 in the Christian year.

Judas Iscariot

Judas came from Kerioth, a village in Judaea, so that he was the only apostle who was not from Galilee. He looked after the money for the band of apostles. He betrayed Jesus for thirty pieces of silver, the price of a slave. Some think that he did this to force Jesus to set up an earthly kingdom, in which Judas would be powerful.

Judas was so grieved for what he had done that he hanged himself. His symbol is a shield of yellow—the colour of despised dung.

Read about Judas in: John 6. 66-71; John 12. 1-8; Matthew 26. 3-5 and 14-16; John 13. 2, 11, 21-30; Mark 14. 32-46; Matthew 27. 1-10; Acts 1. 15-20.

Galilee

Some time after his baptism and temptations Jesus had gone back to Galilee, his homeland. It was in Galilee that he spent most of his ministry. It lasted between two and three years.

We can divide Galilee into three parts. The northern part was called UPPER GALILEE. It is very hilly, with rugged snow-capped mountains, and not many towns. Nazareth, the home town of Jesus, lay in LOWER GALILEE whose gentler hills sloped down to the Plain of Esdraelon. The third part was the SEA OF GALILEE with its many busy fishing-towns and country villages.

Much of Galilee was fertile land, for it was well-watered by the streams flowing from the mountains in the north. On the hill-sides were trees and shrubs, orchards of olives and pomegranates, and vineyard terraces. In the valleys were rich corn-fields and rolling meadows. Both the hills and the plains were dotted with towns and villages humming with life. There were more than 60 towns, for Galilee was well-populated in the time of Jesus.

Its industries were chiefly agriculture and fishing. The busy land was criss-crossed with roads. The great Roman road, THE WAY OF THE SEA, ran through Lower Galilee. It kept the Galileans in close touch with the rest of the world.

Bream

FISHERMEN

At least four of the twelve apostles of Jesus had been fishermen. He called them to become fishers of men.

Fish was a vital food in Palestine and fishing an important industry. Jerusalem had a fish-market, like London's Billingsgate, and a fish-gate into the city. Much of the country's fish came from Galilee both for market and for export. The warm waters of the Sea of Galilee contained 14 different kinds of fish. The most common were carp, perch, bream and the small "St. Peter's fish", 15 to 25 cm long, still popular today. Galilean fishing boats were small. They had one sail and held up to six men.

Fishing

Four ways of catching fish mentioned in the Bible are still used today:

(1) *Spearing* the fish with a harpoon or trident from the shore or from a boat. This is often done at night, holding a torch over the stern of the boat to attract the fish. See Job 41.7.

The Jewish Law forbade eating any fish without scales, such as cat-fish or eels.

Carp   **Perch**   **Cat-fish**

St. Peter's Fish

OF GALILEE

(2) *Casting hook and line* (see Isaiah 19.8; Amos 4.2). Jesus told Peter to catch a fish in this way so that they could pay the half-shekel Temple tax (Matthew 17.27).

(3) *Casting a hand-net*. The fisherman stands close to shore, whirls the net round and flings it into the water in the shape of a cone. Weights sink it and the fish are caught in it (see Matthew 4.17-20).

(4) *Casting a drag-net*. One way of doing this was from a boat, letting the net down, drawing its ends together in a circle, and pulling it into the boat (see Luke 5.4-9). Another way was from the shore, drawing the net in a semicircle (Matthew 13.47-50).

After fishing the precious nets were hung up to dry and carefully mended if necessary.

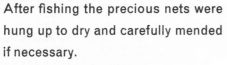

The people of Galilee

The Hebrew name GALILEE means CIRCLE OF THE GENTILES. Now GENTILES means PEOPLES so that by this word the Jews meant all other races. Thus, "Gentiles" really meant "non-Jews" or UNBELIEVERS. Why then should Galilee be called "Land of Unbelievers"?

In Old Testament times Galilee was often invaded. Many of its people were taken away as captives, and foreigners came to settle there. In this way the Galileans became a very mixed people and the Jews of the south often called it GALILEE OF THE GENTILES. It was only about 100 years before the birth of Jesus that the people of Galilee had been made to accept the Jewish religion.

Now the Jews of Judaea in the south were pure Jews. By race they had nothing to do with Gentiles. By religion they would have no contact with Gentiles, either. They looked down on the Galileans as half-castes. They despised them for their rough accent in speech and for their manners, too. These proud Jews of Judaea made up rude sayings about Galilee. "No prophet could come out of Galilee," they said, forgetting some of the prophets of old. "Nothing good could come out of Nazareth," they sneered.

But the Galileans were just as devoted to the Jewish religion as the men of Judaea. They paid their Temple tax and religious dues, and made their annual pilgrimages to the Temple at Jerusalem. The real difference was that the Galileans lived in daily contact with Greeks and Romans. They were broader in their outlook than the narrow-minded Jews of Jerusalem and Judaea.

Jesus came from Galilee. Eleven of his twelve apostles were Galileans. When the Christian Church began in Jerusalem all its members were from Galilee. And when Jerusalem was destroyed by the Romans in A.D. 70 the Rabbis of the city were glad to find refuge in Galilee. In fact they set up their schools in two pagan cities of the Galilee that they had once despised.

The people of Galilee heard Jesus gladly. It was the Jews of Judaea and their rulers who had Jesus put to death.

Cities of Galilee

SEPPHORIS was the town chosen by Herod Antipas as his capital when he began to rule over Galilee. It is not mentioned in the Gospels but Jesus must have known it well, for it was only four miles north of Nazareth where he grew up. When the Romans ordered a census in A.D. 6, the young men of Sepphoris raised a revolt (Acts 5.37). Their leader, a man named Judas, proclaimed: "We have no Lord or Master but God." The Romans destroyed the town. They crucified 2,000 of its men and made an avenue with their crosses on the road leading to the ruins. Sepphoris was soon rebuilt by wood-workers and stone-masons from all over Galilee. Jesus was eleven years old when all this happened. He may have been left in charge of the shop when Joseph went off to work at Sepphoris—perhaps helping to build the aqueduct and the theatre on the hillside the ruins of which can still be seen.

SAFED in Upper Galilee was a town built on a high hill, so that it could be seen for many miles. This was the place Jesus meant when he said, "a city set on a hill cannot be hid" (Matthew 5.14).

CANA was about 8 km from Nazareth. It was a very ancient walled town, with springs of crystal water and groves of pome-granates. It was the home of the apostle Nathanael whom Jesus

GALILEE

Most of the ministry of Jesus was spent in Galilee, his own country, and most
of his followers were Galileans. Many of the events described in the Gospels
took place in these towns and villages of Galilee.

Make your own map of Galilee and add to it the names of towns as you read
about them.

Upper Galilee

PHOENICIA

GALILEE

Chorazin•

•Bethsaida

Capernaum•

Sea
of
Galilee

Magdala•

Cana•

Tiberias•

•Hippos

DECAPOLIS

Nazareth•

Mt.Tabor

•Gadara

R. Jordan

Valley of Esdraelon

Nain•

Sea
of
Galilee

V. of Jezreel

Scythopolis•

•Pella

SAMARIA

Mt.Tabor and Valley of Esdraelon

PERAEA

first saw under one of its many fig-trees (John 1.45-51). It was here, at the wedding-feast of some relatives to which Jesus had been invited, that he turned water into wine. It was here that Jesus was teaching when the nobleman came, asking Jesus to heal his son.

NAIN was a small town in the south of Galilee, some 9 km from Nazareth. It lay on a hill called "Little Hermon". Jesus was once entering the town when he met a funeral procession. The only son of a poor widow had died. A burial-place, always outside the town or village, had to be at least 50 cubits (roughly 22 m) from the nearest house. The body was wrapped in linen and carried there on a litter by the relatives. The women went in front, weeping and wailing aloud. The Hebrew word for this mourning was YALAL, almost suggesting the noise the women made. Jesus was sorry for the widow and restored her son to her.

NAZARETH also comes into the story of Jesus' ministry. One day he went back to his home town. On the sabbath he went to the synagogue service, just as he always did wherever he was. But this was the synagogue where he had been to school as a boy and worshipped each sabbath with Joseph.

The word SYNAGOGUE means a GATHERING OF PEOPLE or a CONGREGATION. In Old Testament times the Jews had been taken away from Jerusalem and made to live as captives in Babylon. They had always worshipped God with sacrifices in the Temple at Jerusalem; but the Law forbade them to make sacrifices anywhere else, lest they should follow heathen ways. Thus in Babylon they had to invent a new kind of worship. They met at first in each other's houses to sing psalms, to say prayers and to read their sacred writings and hear them taught. Then they built churches

SYNAGOGUE AT CAPERNAUM

On the site of Capernaum
have been found the ruins
of a fine white limestone
synagogue. It was built
about 200 years after the
time of Jesus on the ruins
of the one he had used.
It was beautifully decorated.

This carving was a 2nd
century idea of the Tabernacle of the ancient Jews
when they were wanderers
in the time of Moses.

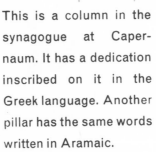

This is a column in the
synagogue at Caper-
naum. It has a dedication
inscribed on it in the
Greek language. Another
pillar has the same words
written in Aramaic.

where they could gather or congregate for worship. These were the synagogues.

Many Jews never went back to Palestine. By the time of Jesus they lived all over the world, wherever their business took them, chiefly in the big cities. Those who could made a pilgrimage to Jerusalem, but that was only once a year at the most. All the rest of the time, the Jews, both in Palestine and abroad, worshipped God in their local synagogues.

It needed only 10 Jewish men to form a new synagogue. In the towns there were many. In Jerusalem there were about 500, many of them for Jews from abroad. Each synagogue had a committee or Council to run it and up to three "rulers", one of whom presided. The synagogue was used for worship, for school, for meetings and for a lawcourt. Services were held every day—especially on Monday and Thursday which were market days.

The chief service was of course on Saturday, the sacred sabbath. It lasted about an hour. It began with the singing of a psalm and then everyone joined in the Shema. After the prayers everyone said in a loud voice AMEN—SO BE IT, making the prayers their own. The main lesson was read from one of the Law Books of the Scriptures. These were written in Hebrew, so the lesson was translated into Aramaic in case anyone had forgotten the Hebrew he had learnt at school. Then came more psalms and prayers.

The last lesson was taken from one of the Books of Prophets, the second part of the Hebrew Bible (which is our Old Testament). On this day at Nazareth Jesus was invited to read it. He was handed the scroll by the HAZZAN—the official who taught the boys, looked after the synagogue and arranged the services. Jesus read his three verses from the Book of Isaiah. Then he handed the scroll back and, as the custom was, sat down to speak about it. "I am fulfilling that prophecy," Jesus said, "God has filled me with his Spirit. He has sent me to preach the Good News that his Kingdom has come."

SCROLL OF THE BOOK OF ISAIAH

This is one of the scrolls found in a cave by the Dead Sea, the library of the monks called Essenes. This very scroll was being used in the time of Jesus. (See also p. 40-41). In the synagogue at Nazareth he would have read from one exactly like it.

At first the townsfolk of Nazareth were awed by the fine words of Jesus. Then they realised what he was saying. "Isn't this Yeshua bar Joseph, the wood-worker?" they muttered to each other. "Who does he think he is? We know all about him. Why, we've watched him grow up. He mended our tools for us!" They grew more and more angry. Jesus calmly went on, "No prophet is welcomed by his

116

own people," he said, "It has always been like that. That is why Elijah the prophet went to help a foreign woman of Phoenicia. That is why Elisha the prophet healed a pagan of Syria of his leprosy."

Jesus got no further. The service should have ended with a

The pen used for writing on papyrus or parchment was called a CALAMUS or REED. The reed was shaped and then a slit was made at the tip to hold ink—like our split nibs today.

This bronze pen that has been found is much more pointed than a reed pen.

INK-POT AND PEN

Black ink was made with soot and gun,. Water was added to the powder when ink was needed. The inkpot was made of wood or, like this one, of metal. A scribe carried his box of ink tied to his girdle. Red ink **was** made from ochre.

blessing. That day it ended in a riot. The men of Nazareth crowded around Jesus as he walked out, shouting and waving their fists at him. They followed him up the hill he knew so well until he disappeared in the caves.

Jesus never went back to Nazareth. It was only because of him that it ever became famous.

Cities by the sea of Galilee

In the time of Jesus, the great Sea of Galilee was covered with sails. Around it were twelve towns and many more villages. It was a busy, thriving district with a big fish industry. Fish was a staple food of the people of Palestine, and fish from Galilee were famous. Much of a fisherman's catch was salted, for it quickly turned bad in the heat. The town of Magdala had another name—TARICHAEA or PICKLE-TOWN, for it was famous for its fish-salting as well as its shipbuilding. Fish exports from Galilee went as far away as Spain. In Rome itself people ate a popular dish called "muries" ("salt-fish") from the Sea of Galilee. Many of its other towns had "fishy" names, too. MAGDALA means DRIED FISHES, for example, and BETHSAIDA means HOUSE OF FISHERS.

Fishermen clubbed together to buy their boats and nets. They worked together in a group of about six men, with one of them as leader. The four apostles, Andrew, Simon Peter, James and John, worked together with Peter as their leader. They shared the money from the sale of their fish.

Fishermen of Galilee were strong in body and character, and in spirit, too. That was why Jesus gave Simon a new name—PETER which means ROCK, just as he nicknamed James and John SONS OF THUNDER. They were brave and hearty—just the kind he wanted to become his "fishers of men". Jesus had known them for a long time and knew their good qualities. Perhaps he had made their boats for them when he had been a wood-worker.

Jesus had another reason for calling these fishermen. They were devout, God-fearing men. Andrew had been a disciple of John the Baptist, and he had brought his brother Simon to Jesus. James and

118

John were sons of Salome, probably the sister of Jesus' mother. They were the kind of men to give their hearts to a prophet.

CAPERNAUM was the town Jesus chose as his headquarters. He knew it well and he had often been there with his family. It was a good centre for his work. It lay on the north-west shore of the Sea of Galilee. The Romans had a garrison there, for the main road from Damascus in Syria to the far north ran through Capernaum down to Jerusalem and on to Egypt in the south. The Roman officer in charge of the garrison was a devout man, well liked by the Jews. He had even built them a synagogue. It was they who asked Jesus to heal his servant.

119

THE SYNAGOGUE

In 1905 scholars began to explore the ruins of the ancient synagogue at Capernaum. Some think it was the synagogue in which Jesus taught (John 6. 59, for example) and which had been built for the Jews by a devout Roman officer (Luke 7.1-5). But most think that it is a later synagogue built about A.D. 200. But it is certainly on the site of the synagogue Jesus knew.

Exterior

The earlier synagogue on this site had been built by a Roman officer stationed at Capernaum.

Luke tells us that it was his servant whom Jesus healed (Luke 7.1-10). Jesus marvelled at the great faith of this Roman, and gladly granted his request.

Roman Centurion

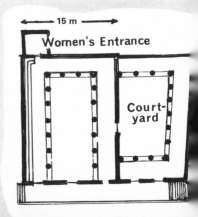

15 m

Women's Entrance

Court-yard

AT CAPERNAUM (see also p. 114)

Scholars have made drawings showing what the synagogue must have looked like both outside and inside. It ran from north to south and faced Jerusalem. It had terraces, climbed by steps, and it was paved with limestone. It had four doors, one leading to the enclosed courtyard on the right. There would be a fountain in it for worshippers to wash hands and feet before entering.

It was in the earlier building on this very site that Jesus taught and healed (Mark 1. 21-28; Luke 6. 6-12).

As an important centre of communications Capernaum also had its customs house. One of the tax-collectors, Matthew Levi, knew Jesus well and he was all ready when Jesus came and called him to be one of his disciples.

Jesus made his home at Capernaum. He lived in the house of Simon Peter who was married and had his mother-in-law, as well as his brother Andrew, living with him. Crowds often gathered at the door, seeking Jesus.

Sometimes Jesus taught in the house, sometimes in the synagogue, sometimes from a boat near the shore and sometimes on the hillside. He was very popular in those early days of his ministry.

TIBERIAS was the city which Herod Antipas made into his new capital after Sepphoris. He named it after Tiberius, the Roman Emperor, to honour him. He built it on the ruins of an ancient town which included a cemetery. This made it "unclean" to the Jews and they would not enter it. It was a pagan city, too, in its ways. Herod's court lived there in luxury by its hot springs, which are still famous today. Jesus must have known the city well but he never went into it.

BETHSAIDA or "House of Fishers" must have been a popular name, for there were two places called this. The larger one, on the north shore of the Sea of Galilee, was called BETHSAIDA JULIAS. Philip, who ruled in this part of Palestine, named it after Julia, the daughter of the Emperor Augustus. This was the home of Philip the apostle, and the brothers Andrew and Simon Peter came from Bethsaida Julias, too. It was just outside this town that Jesus healed a blind man. It was on a hillside nearby that he fed the 5,000 people.

THE CAPERNAUM CUSTOMS OFFICE

Capernaum was an important road centre and the Romans made it one of their headquarters. It had its own garrison and its own customs house. You can read how the Romans collected taxes on page 24.

Matthew Levi sat at the customs house collecting taxes until Jesus called him. A Roman soldier would often be standing by to see that there was no trouble.
You can read how Jesus called Matthew in Luke 5. 27-32.

CHORAZIN, on the north-west shore, was another town where Jesus taught and healed. It was famous for the fine wheat grown on the fertile fields nearby. The ruins of its synagogue have been found and you can see a picture of its "Moses' Seat" on page 34. Jesus condemned the people of both Chorazin and Bethsaida for not accepting the Good News of God's kingdom.

MAGDALA lay on the west shore, north of Tiberias. It was famous, as we saw, for its salt-fishing and boat-building. It is famous to us because of the woman disciple who came from it—Mary of Magdala or Mary Magdalene. You can read in John 20. 1-18 the lovely story of how she first saw Jesus after he had risen from the dead.

GADARA lay on the east of the Sea of Galilee. Here there were two Greek cities of the league called Decapolis. Gadara was seven miles from the Sea and Gerasa was some 32 km away. Each city controlled the territory round about. It seems that the territory of Gadara ran as far as the Sea of Galilee. It was here that Jesus healed the madman who lived in the tombs.

The Greeks cut their tombs out of the rock. They were quite roomy so that they easily gave shelter, especially to an exile cast out by his own people. A herd of pigs nearby was stampeded by the ravings of the lunatic. As Jesus healed him, the pigs rushed madly over the steep rock into the Sea of Galilee. In ancient times it was believed that madness was caused by evil spirits. Naturally everyone thought that the evil spirits had gone out of the madman and into the pigs, making them crazy instead.

Jews would not mind the loss of the pigs. The Law taught that pigs were "unclean" animals and Jews would have nothing to do with them. But Gentiles made good money from pig-keeping. Pork was a popular meat with them. Much of it was salted and sold to the Romans for the troops. This was a serious loss to them and they asked Jesus to leave their country, fearing his strange powers.

A BRONZE PIG

This was found at Pompeii, a Roman city in Italy which was covered with lava from Mount Vesuvius in A.D. 79 Jews were forbidden by their Law from having anything to do with pigs. This may have been because of the dirty habits of pigs, which often led to skin diseases. But it was more likely because swine were sacred to pagan religions. The Romans often used pigs for their sacrifices. Read Leviticus 11.7; Matthew 7.6; Luke 15.11-32. For a proverb about the sow see 2 Peter 2.22.

Caves were used for burial, or tombs were cut in the limestone rock. The valley outside Jerusalem was particularly popular for burials, and many tombs have been found there. This was because the Jews believed that the Messiah would come back to earth there. Tombs like this gave good shelter.

A TOMB CUT IN ROCK NEAR JERUSALEM

Parables

The Gospels often tell us how Jesus travelled around the towns and villages of Galilee, teaching in the synagogues, preaching the Good News of the coming of God's kingdom, and healing the sick. He showed men the rule of God in his words and in his deeds.

The people of Galilee liked listening to Jesus. His teaching was fresh and new—not like the dry-as-dust teaching of the Scribes. He spoke to them simply. He told stories of everyday life, he drew lessons from things they could see around them.

"Look at that sower, up there on the hillside, scattering seed," he once said, "Watch where it falls. . . ." (Mark 4. 3-9). Another time he said, "Look at that flock of birds. God provides food for them, doesn't he? Just think how much more he must care for you. So don't worry about food and clothes. . ." (Matthew 6.26). Again, he said, "Look at the beauty of those wild-flowers on the hill-side. God clothed them in their beauty. Will he not much more clothe you?. . ." (Matthew 6.28-33).

In his stories Jesus was comparing life in the kingdom of God with life in Palestine. Often his stories began, "The kingdom of God is like. . ." That is why we call his stories PARABLES which means COMPARISONS. Sometimes they were complete stories. Sometimes they were picture sayings such as "You are the light of the world" or "You are the salt of the earth" (Matthew 5.13-14).

From these stories we can learn how people lived in Galilee in the time of Jesus. But Jesus told them to teach what the kingdom of God was like and to win men to it.

Miracles

Jesus also made the kingdom of God known in his deeds. He showed the rule of God over sickness and over nature. When men saw the power of God at work in these deeds they should have believed in the Good News of Jesus.

We call these deeds of Jesus MIRACLES. This comes from the Roman word MIRACULUM which means a WONDER. But Jesus did not expect people to wonder at his deeds. He expected them to turn to God. The Gospels were written in Greek and the Greek words for these deeds of Jesus really mean SIGNS and WORKS OF POWER. They were signs of God's kingdom and power at work among men.

That is why it is wrong to think of these deeds of Jesus simply as wonders. In his temptations he had refused to win men to God by doing wonders. These deeds were done out of sympathy for those who suffered. When Jesus had healed people he told them not to tell anyone; but they could not keep such secrets and his fame spread all over Galilee.

Jesus in Galilee

Our large maps of the land of Jesus make it seem that it was a big country and that distances would therefore be great. But it is a tiny country and the distances Jesus travelled were really small. All the towns we have mentioned were within 32 km of Capernaum, where Jesus made his home in Galilee.

Jesus travelled through the countryside on foot, walking with his disciples from one town or village to the next. But the fishermen's boats were very useful, too. Often he crossed the Sea of Galilee in one of their boats to get from one place to another—or even to get away from the crowds. Fierce storms occur quite suddenly on the Sea of Galilee, without any warning at all. They are caused by differences of temperature between the land round the Sea and the inland hills. The winds swoop down over the mountains which protect the shore and lash the waters further out. That was why fishing was mostly done at night in order to avoid the storms. Jesus travelled at the northern end of the Sea and here there was no high land to protect the water. He and his disciples were sometimes caught in such storms. You can read about one in Mark 4.35-41. The smaller fishing boats could easily be swamped by the huge waves and even the fishermen were terrified.

The fame of Jesus grew during his journeying in Galilee and he became very popular. Soon his twelve apostles could be sent out in pairs to preach the Good News, to cast out devils, and to heal the sick. Jesus gave them careful instructions (Mark 6.7-13). They were to be like fishermen, drawing souls into the net of God's kingdom, or like shepherds seeking lost sheep, or like labourers gathering in the harvest.

One thing about Jesus struck everyone. He spoke with authority. He did not begin,—"Rabbi So-and-so says. . .". He always began, "I say unto you." It was just as if he spoke directly from God. In his deeds, too, God was seen at work, showing his authority over disease and over nature. No wonder many people believed in Jesus. Some of them even began to think of the prophecies of the Messiah. Could Jesus of Nazareth be the Christ?

Once a big crowd got very excited. There seemed to be thousands of people. Peter told the story to Mark, who wrote it down carefully

in his Gospel. Peter remembered that it was in the spring and the grass was green; and when the brightly-dressed people sat down in groups, it seemed to Peter that they looked like colourful flower-beds in a tidy garden, with the green grass between each group. A lad offered his lunch to Jesus to help to feed them. It was only five little flat loaves and two small fishes; but Jesus blessed it and fed the people with it. Then they remembered one of the prophecies of the Messiah—how he would feed the people (Isaiah 25.6). John, in his gospel, tells us that the crowd shouted for Jesus and wanted to crown him as their king (John 6.1-15); but Jesus managed to get away from them and hid from them in the hills. He was not that kind of Messiah.

Jesus spent busy days in Galilee. There were always people seeking him. He gave himself to them in words and in deeds. It must have made him very tired. Yet he would often get up early in the morning and go out to be alone. Sometimes he even stayed out alone all night. This was the secret of his strength. For when he went out he was not alone. He was with his heavenly Father. It was being with God that gave him his strength, his authority and his power during those hot, dusty days in Galilee.

The feeding of the 5,000 people is the only miracle story told in each of the four Gospels. This shows its importance. The boy would have brought his lunch in a basket or in a satchel. The five loaves were round and flat, like our pancakes. They were made of coarse brown bread. You can read how bread was baked on page 79. The two small fishes would have come from the Sea of Galilee—one of the kinds mentioned on page 108-109.

A biography to plan

Find and read these stories of John the Baptist:

His birth	Luke 1. 5-24 and 57-80.
His appearance	Mark 1. 4-8.
His preaching	Luke 3. 3-18.
Who he was	John 1. 19-28.
His witness to Jesus	John 1. 29-31.
His baptising	John 1.28; 3.23; 10.40.
His disciples	Luke 7.18; 11.1; 5.33.
His imprisonment	Matthew 11. 2-6.
His death	Mark 6.14-29.
What Jesus thought of him	Matthew 11. 7-19.

Now you can write your own life story of John the Baptist, with a map and your own pictures. Reference books will help, too.

To look up

Look up in the Old Testament these three prophecies of the Messiah:

Isaiah 25.6; Daniel 7.13; Isaiah 9.6. The three temptations of Jesus came from them. Find the answers Jesus made to each temptation in: Deuteronomy 8.3, 6.16 and 6.13.

To map

Make your own map of Galilee, adding to it the names of places as you read about them. Under the name of each town, you can list the things which happened there if you make your map large enough.

To discuss
Why did Jesus refuse to be the kind of Messiah people wanted? What was wrong with the three ways he rejected?

To read
You can read the prophecies of the Suffering Servant of God in Isaiah 42.1-9; 49. 1-6; 50.4-9; 52.13-53.12. What verses remind you of Jesus?

A chart to make
Make your own chart of the twelve apostles. It should show all we know about their homes, their work, their symbols, and what tradition says happened to them.

To research
Choose one of the twelve apostles and find out all you can about him. You will need reference books as well as your Bible. Then write a newspaper article telling your readers all we know about him. Do not forget that each apostle has a special day in the Christian Year. You could find the prayer for that day and include it in your story.

A class project to work out
The whole class can work in groups on a project on Galilee. The topics for the groups will be: geography, climate, agriculture, dress, towns, roads, villages, fishing. Reference books will be helpful. Your articles, stories, maps and drawings should make a fine wall display. Bible references for towns are given below.

Questions to answer

Why did Jesus begin his ministry in A.D. 28?

What had John the Baptist to do with the Messiah?

What were the three temptations of Jesus? What did they mean?

Why did Jesus choose twelve apostles?

What differences were there between the Galileans and the Jews of Judaea?

What happened at a synagogue service?—usually, or at one in particular?

Why was Jesus cast out from Nazareth?

Why did Jesus make Capernaum his headquarters?

Why did Jesus become popular with the people of Galilee?

What are "Parables"?

What do we mean by "Miracles"?

To draw or model

Make drawings or models of the boats and nets used by the fishermen on the Sea of Galilee.

To imagine

Imagine you were a newspaper reporter either at (a) Capernaum on the sabbath described in Mark 1.21-34; or at (b) Nazareth on the sabbath described in Luke 4.16-29. Write an account for your paper of what happened, and what everyone thought about these happenings.

To discuss

Why was Jesus so popular with the people of Galilee?

To choose

Here are the Gospel references for the towns of Galilee. Choose one and tell your own story of what happened there. As you have spare time you can write about others, too.

Cana   John 2. 1-11; John 4.46-53; John 21.2.
Nain   Luke 7.11-17.
Nazareth   John 1.46; Luke 4.16-29.
Bethsaida   John 1.44; Mark 8.22-26.
Gadara   Mark 5.1-20.

A class study to do

Since Jesus made Capernaum his headquarters in Galilee many events took place there. Here are the Gospel references for them: John 2.12; Matthew 4.12-13 and 9.1; Mark 1.21-34; Mark 2.1-17; Mark 3.1-6; Mark 3.31-35; Luke 7.1-10; Matthew 17.24-27.

Each group can take one event and write its own story with pictures and models and maps. One group will need to find out about Capernaum itself. Reference books will help too.

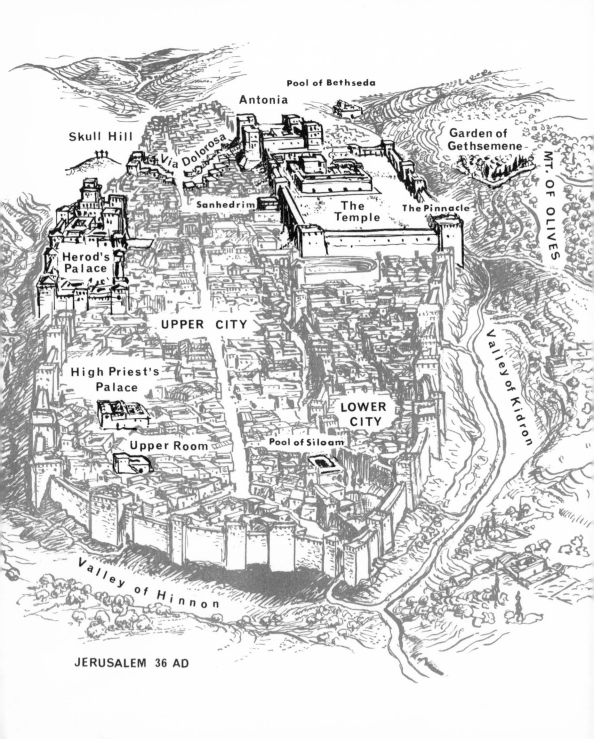

Skull Hill

Via Dolorosa

Antonia

Pool of Bethseda

Garden of Gethsemene

MT. OF OLIVES

Sanhedrim

The Temple

The Pinnacle

Herod's Palace

UPPER CITY

High Priest's Palace

LOWER CITY

Valley of Kidron

Upper Room

Pool of Siloam

Valley of Hinnon

JERUSALEM 36 AD

Jerusalem

Enemies in Galilee

Jesus grew very popular with the people of Galilee. He went all round their towns and villages, teaching and healing. He showed them the love of God in his words, in his deeds, and above all in himself. He sent out his twelve apostles, too, so that more and more people could hear the Good News of God's love and forgiveness.

The crowds gathered wherever Jesus went. Some of them really believed in him. Some followed him out of curiosity. Some only went for what they could get out of him. But none of the common people turned against Jesus. It was the important people who turned against Jesus. The more popular he became the more suspicious they grew.

Chief among them were the Scribes and Pharisees. The Scribes were teachers of the sacred Law of God. The Pharisees lived strictly by the Law, keeping every detail of it. Jesus broke the Law. He even spoke against it and sometimes put his words in place of it. He went to parties given by people who were condemned by the Law—tax collectors and other sinners, like Matthew Levi. He did not go without food on the appointed days, for he preferred to fast secretly. Worst of all, Jesus broke the laws of the Sabbath, God's holy day, in order to do good to those in need.

The Scribes and Pharisees looked down on the Jews of Galilee. Few of them lived in Galilee and they did not have much power

135

there. Most of them lived in Judaea in the south, especially in Jerusalem; but even there they heard of the new prophet in Galilee and of his growing popularity. The Sadducees of Jerusalem heard about him, too. They kept on good terms with the Romans in order to preserve their power and wealth. Galilee was always a trouble spot. Every now and then some peasant set himself up as the Messiah and raised a revolt against Rome. This carpenter of Nazareth looked like another of them.

Soon, picked men were hurrying north to Galilee to find out about this new prophet. They were clever Pharisees and Sadducees. They followed Jesus about, they watched him closely, they questioned him, they tried to make him look foolish in front of the people; but it was they who looked foolish when Jesus answered them. Worse still, he spoke against them to the crowds around him.

No wonder the Pharisees grew to hate Jesus. They found allies in the Herodians—the followers of King Herod who ruled over Galilee. Herod was a sly, suspicious man. Jesus called him a "fox". He was superstitious, too. He had put John the Baptist to death. When he heard about the new prophet, Jesus of Nazareth, he was afraid it was John the Baptist come back from the dead.

Herod was hated and despised by the people of Galilee. He knew it, and he was afraid of anyone else becoming too popular. No wonder he wanted to get hold of Jesus.

Tyre and Sidon
Jesus was now in danger of being arrested by Herod's men. He left Herod's territory and went with his apostles to the north-west.

Soon they were in the land of the Phoenicians, out of Herod's reach. The land belonging to Tyre and Sidon, the two great cities of the Phoenicians, stretched as far as Galilee. It was only 64 km from Galilee to these two great sea-ports. They were bustling with traders and busy with ships that sailed all over the world—even to far-away Cornwall, in wild Britain, to barter cloth for precious tin.

Jesus and his apostles were safe among these foreigners. He wanted peace and quiet and it is unlikely that he visited the noisy cities.

But no sooner had Jesus come to the borders of Phoenicia than a woman cried out after him. She must have heard of the popular Jewish prophet. She cried out after Jesus to heal her daughter who

A PHOENICIAN WOMAN

In Sidon were found the Royal Tombs of the city's rulers. This woman comes from one of the carved stone coffins, called the Sarcophagus of the Weeping Women. Her face shows she is Phoenician but her dress is Greek. This tomb dates from the fourth century B.C. But the woman who came to Jesus must have looked very much like her.

suffered from fits. She fell at his feet, refusing to go away. Jesus spoke to her in a proverb. "It is wrong to take food from the children and to give it to the puppies from the streets," he said. "True, Lord", the woman replied, "But the household pets eat the tit-bits which fall from the family table."

Jesus rewarded the great faith of the woman and healed her daughter. Perhaps, too, he admired her clever reply. Like many of the Phoenicians, she lived by Greek customs. The Jews despised dogs and never kept them as pets. They became hungry, snarling scavengers of the streets. But the Greeks were fond of their dogs, especially hunting dogs. At meal-times they tied their pets under the couches on which they lay to eat.

Jesus did not mean that foreigners were "dogs", even if he did use the word for "puppies" or "pets". He meant that he had come to the Jewish people—the children of God. Several stories tell how he helped foreigners who had faith in him.

GREEK PET DOGS

It was the Greek and Roman custom to recline at meals on sloping couches. The Greeks tied their pet dogs under the couches at mealtime, where they ate the tit-bits dropped for them. This illustration, from a Greek bowl of the seventh century B.C., pictures the feast at the wedding of a princess.

DOGS IN THE BIBLE

There were two kinds of dogs among the Jews. The first was the shepherd dog, imported from abroad, used to guard and to guide the sheep (see Job 30.1).

Much more common were the scavenger dogs of the streets. They are mentioned over 40 times in the Bible. They were never kept as pets and they lived off rubbish. They were half-starved, snarly, vicious but cowardly. It was a terrible insult to call anyone "a dog", "son of a dog", or "dead dog". "Give not that which is holy to the dogs" was a proverb.

These references will show what dogs were like: Exodus 22.31; Matthew 7.6 and 15.26; Isaiah 56.10-11; Psalm 59.6 and 14; Proverbs 26.11; Deuteronomy 23.18; Proverbs 26.17; Psalm 22. 20.

Caesarea Philippi

When Jesus returned to Galilee the Pharisees and Sadducees were waiting for him. He went to the other side of the Sea of Galilee in a fishing-boat. There he was safe in the territory of King Philip. He and his apostles set out on foot to the north. They climbed the hills which led to the great Mount Hermon. It is 548 m above the Sea of Galilee and it rises to 2743 m above sea-level. Because it is so high, the top of Mount Hermon is covered with snow all the year round. The River Jordan comes from its melting snows.

The river begins in a cave. In ancient times the cave was sacred to the Greek god Pan. In the cliffs round about can still be seen the niches which held statues of the god. The town that grew up here, about 200 B.C. was called Paneas—Pan's Place. King Philip rebuilt

THE CAVE AT
CAESAREA PHILIPPI

the town in the time of Jesus. He gave it a new name in honour of the Roman Emperor, Tiberius Caesar. He called it Caesarea. But it was always known as CAESAREA PHILIPPI or PHILIP'S CAESAREA. That was because there was another city named Caesarea, by the Mediterranean Sea, which had been built by Philip's father, Herod the Great. Philip made his new town into a capital for the hot months of summer.

Jesus and his apostles were unknown here. They could find peace and quiet. It was here that Jesus asked the twelve what people thought about him. They told him that some people, like King Herod, thought that he was John the Baptist come back to life; and that other people thought that he was Elijah, or Jeremiah, or one of the other great prophets of the past, come back to earth. Then Jesus asked them directly, "Who do you think I am?" It was bluff Simon Peter who blurted it out, "We believe that you are the Messiah—the Christ," he said.

Jesus was glad when Simon made his GREAT CONFESSION, as it is called. It was now that he gave Simon his second name. In the Aramaic language which they spoke, it was CEPHAS, a word which also meant ROCK. In the Greek language in which the Gospels were written it was PETROS, from which we get our word PETER, and that also meant ROCK. Still today in the French language the word PIERRE means both PETER and ROCK.

Jesus was glad that his apostles knew who he was, for now he could teach them more. He began by warning them to keep it a secret. People must not think that he was the Messiah they looked for—a Saviour who would bring them prosperity and miracles and power. Then he went on, "You know the Scriptures. They tell how the Messiah will bring peace and righteousness and love. They tell how he will be thrown out and put to death, and how he will rise from the dead."

The apostles were horrified. They thought they were going to share in the glorious kingdom of God—and Jesus was talking about suffering and dying! Again it was Peter who spoke up. They could not bear to think of their beloved Master suffering. He must be wrong. But Jesus answered him sternly. Then he patiently went on trying to make them understand what must happen.

Mount Hermon

Jesus spent some days with his apostles in the quiet hills. Then, one day, he took Peter and James and John and they climbed the foothills of Mount Hermon. Jesus went some way ahead of them to pray, but the three tired apostles were soon asleep. They awoke suddenly and looked up. They saw Jesus against the mountain snow. His raiment was white and glistening, and the glory of God seemed all around him. With him they made out two other figures, Moses and Elijah—the two greatest prophets of all, both of whom had left the earth in a mysterious way. And out of the cloud of God's glory there came a voice, saying "This is my beloved Son."

Then, just as suddenly, the three apostles were alone with Jesus. They were frightened by the vision they had seen and they did not know what to say. As they came down the mountain with Jesus he told them to tell no one what they had seen until he had risen from the dead. That was even more mysterious. What could he mean by "rising from the dead" they asked each other.

142

Samaria

Jesus came back to Galilee, but he tried to keep his presence there a secret from Herod's spies. His great aim was to go to Jerusalem, for it was there that everything had to be decided. He must not be kept in Galilee.

Jesus travelled south through Samaria. This was the direct route from Galilee in the north to Judaea in the south, but very few Jews went that way. They took the longer route along by the river Jordan. For centuries there had been enmity between the Jews and the Samaritans. No good Jew would have anything to do with them, if he could avoid it.

Jesus was rejected by the people of one village, but at another he healed ten men who were lepers. Only one came back to say "thank you," and he was a Samaritan.

Jesus had travelled through Samaria at least once before. He had sat and talked with a Samaritan woman at Jacob's Well, which can still be seen today. Jews despised Samaritans because

JACOB'S WELL IN SAMARIA

It was here that Jesus sat and asked the woman of Samaria for a drink of water (John 4.5-12). Still today its water is cool and fresh. The top of the well is 68 cm in diameter. John says that it was "deep". It is 25 m in depth now and it may have been even deeper in the time of Jesus.

they were not pure Jews. Since their quarrel, the Samaritans had built their temple on Mount Gerizim and they worshipped God there—as the few who are still left do today. The Samaritan woman reminded Jesus that her people worshipped on Mount Gerizim, but that the Jews said God could only be worshipped at Jerusalem. Jesus told her that God could be worshipped anywhere, for God is spirit.

Jesus left the unfriendly Samaritans and crossed over to the eastern side of the river Jordan. The land on the east of the river was called PERAEA. It was there that John the Baptist had preached and baptised. Jesus stayed there for some time. It was there that he sent out seventy disciples to carry the Good News to neighbouring villages.

The Feast of Tabernacles

The ministry of Jesus lasted from two to three years. We cannot be sure how often he visited Jerusalem during that time. The first three Gospels, which are very much alike, tell us mostly about Jesus in Galilee. They tell of Jesus visiting Jerusalem only twice. The first visit was when he was a boy. The other was when he went to suffer and die.

Every Jewish man was expected to go to Jerusalem as a pilgrim for the three great feasts of the year. So it is very likely that Jesus went more often. John's Gospel tells mostly about the ministry of Jesus in Judaea. It describes two visits which Jesus made to Jerusalem during this time.

The first was for the Feast of Tabernacles. This came in the autumn, in early October. It was the harvest festival of grapes and olives

144

and other fruits. The feast began when all the fruit had been crushed in the wine-press and the precious juices stored in jars and skins.

The feast lasted for one week. In Jerusalem worshippers offered their gifts at the altar in the Temple. But everyone kept the feast in the home. During it, people slept out of doors in TABERNACLES or TENT-HOUSES, or in BOOTHS which were made of leafy branches. Tents and booths were set up in the courtyards or on the flat roofs of the houses. Streets were decorated, too.

The Feast of Tabernacles was to thank God for the fruit harvest. But it had another purpose, too. The tents and booths were to remind the Jews that their ancestors, in the time of Moses, had wandered for many years in the wilderness. They had no land of their own, and only tents or booths for homes. So this Feast helped the Jews to remember that, whether they were wanderers or settlers, they depended upon God for the food which gave them life.

John's Gospel says that Jesus went secretly to Jerusalem for this Feast. He stayed at the village of Bethany, just 3 km from the city, with his friends—Mary and Martha and their brother Lazarus. Still today it is called "The Village of Lazarus".

Towards the middle of the week Jesus went into the Temple and taught openly. The well-educated Jews of the city were astonished that this peasant carpenter of Nazareth could speak so well. The Pharisees and Sadducees sent men to arrest Jesus, but they came back without him. "No one ever spoke like him," they said. One of the Pharisees spoke up for Jesus. His name was Nicodemus. He had been to talk with Jesus secretly at night-time and he believed in him, though he did not have the courage to say so openly. "Does our law condemn a man without even knowing what he has done?"

he said, timidly. The proud priests soon silenced him. "No prophet could come out of Galilee," they sneered.

The Feast of Dedication

Two months later Jesus visited Jerusalem again. It was for the FEAST OF DEDICATION, early in December. This Feast celebrated a great victory. In 165 B.C. a brilliant Jewish leader, named Judas the Hammerer (Maccabaeus), had won back Jerusalem from the pagans. He had thrown out their heathen idols and he had re-dedicated the Temple for the worship of God. Ever after, the Jews kept the Feast of Dedication to honour his triumph.

It was also called the FEAST OF LIGHTS, for all the lamps were lit in Jewish homes, torch-light processions went through the streets, and the Temple itself was ablaze with lights. It was probably at this time that Jesus said "I am the light of the world."

Jesus taught in Solomon's Porch—the cloisters which led to the Court of the Gentiles. The Jews asked him, "Tell us openly if you really are the Christ." Jesus said "I and my Father are one." The Jews shouted, "You are making yourself one with God! Blasphemy! You must die!" The punishment for blasphemy was stoning to death and the angry Jews snatched up stones to kill Jesus; but Jesus escaped from them and went back to Peraea beyond Jordan.

Jesus was not running away when he left Galilee to avoid Herod's men, or when he left Jerusalem to avoid the Jewish leaders. He was waiting for the right moment. Then he would make his open claim to be the promised Saviour. It had to be at Jerusalem, the sacred capital of the Jews where stood God's holy Temple. That was why Jesus avoided being arrested by Herod in Galilee. It had to be

146

at the right time, the most sacred time of the whole Jewish year.

That time was the Feast of the Passover.

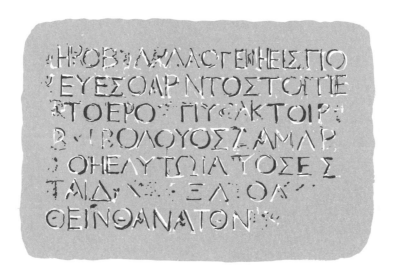

THE TEMPLE WARNING TO GENTILES

This stone inscription was found in 1870. It stood in the Court of the Gentiles and warned them, on pain of death, not to go any further into the Inner Court. It reads:

LET NO ONE OF THE GENTILES ENTER INSIDE THE BARRIER AROUND THIS SANCTUARY AND THE PORCH AND IF HE TRANSGRESSES HE SHALL HIMSELF BEAR THE BLAME FOR HIS ENSUING DEATH.

This inscription was written in Greek, the common language of the world of that time. There was also a Latin version beside it.

PLAN OF THE TEMPLE AT JERUSALEM

Herod the Great had rebuilt Jerusalem and he decided to enlarge and beautify the Temple to match his fine city. This would also please his Jewish subjects, he hoped.

He began the work in 20 B.C. But only specially trained priests could work on the sacred site and the building went on for years. It was not, in fact, complete when the Temple was finally destroyed, during bitter fighting with the Romans, on August 10th in the year A.D. 70.

The Temple area was about 457 m by 304 m and surrounded with a strong, towered wall.

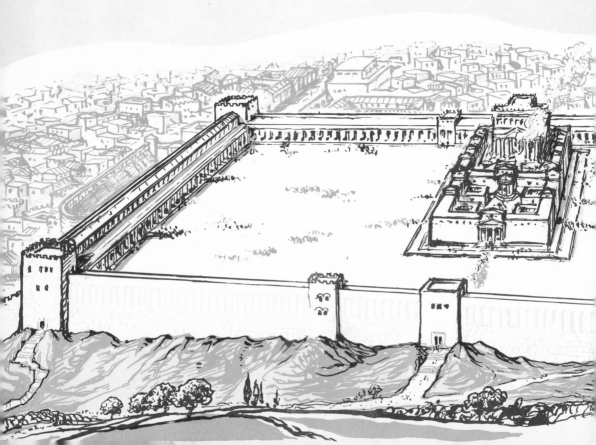

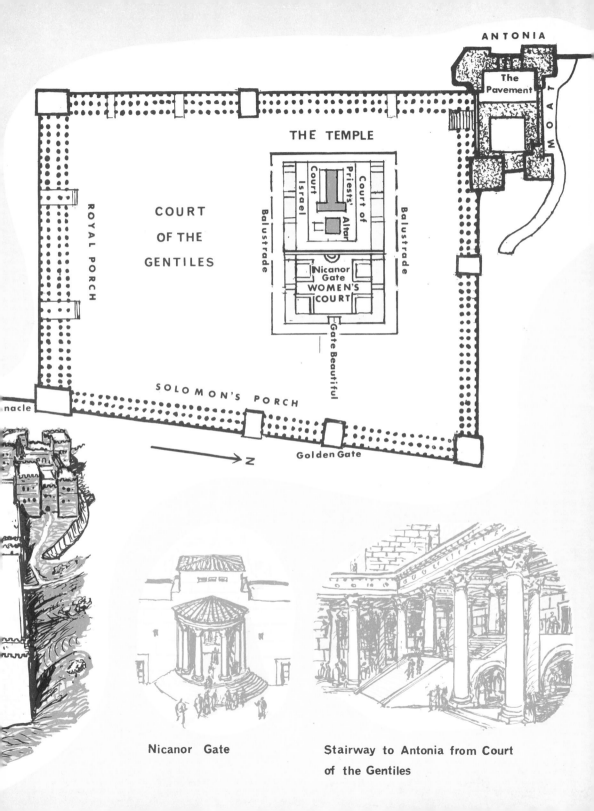

ANTONIA

The Pavement

MOAT

THE TEMPLE

Court of Israel

Court of Priests'

Altar

Balustrade

Balustrade

Nicanor Gate

WOMEN'S COURT

Gate Beautiful

COURT

OF THE

GENTILES

ROYAL PORCH

SOLOMON'S PORCH

nacle

→ N

Golden Gate

Nicanor Gate

Stairway to Antonia from Court of the Gentiles

The Feast of the Passover

Jesus was safe in Peraea, teaching and healing. But John's Gospel tells how one day a message came to Jesus from his friends at Bethany. Lazarus, the brother of Martha and Mary, was very ill. The disciples were worried when Jesus said that he was going to Bethany, for the Jews would try to seize him if they knew. But Jesus went. Lazarus had already died by the time he reached Bethany. Jesus brought him back to life.

Spies took the news back to Jerusalem. The leaders of the Pharisees and Sadducees held a hurried meeting. They were soon agreed — Jesus must die. He threatened their beliefs, their wealth, and their power. He was becoming too popular. Soon he would raise a revolt against Rome. Then the Romans, tired of Jewish rebellions, might take all power from the Jews and rule the country themselves. They might even destroy the whole Jewish people. The high priest gave his decision: "We cannot allow our nation to perish," he said. "We can save our people only by getting rid of this Jesus. It is quite fitting that one man should die so that the people may live."

Spies were sent out to find where Jesus was and to arrest him: but he went away to a lonely village, high up in the hills, waiting till his time should come.

Then, at last, Passover time drew near. Jesus set out on his last journey to Jerusalem. When he came to Jericho the crowds flocked to see the popular prophet. The chief tax collector, named Zacchaeus, was a little man. He climbed up a fig-mulberry tree by the roadside and peered down through the leafy branches. How astonished he was when Jesus stopped and looked up at him and

spoke kindly to him! Jesus went to dinner at the house of Zacchaeus and Zacchaeus' whole life was changed.

Coming out of Jericho, Jesus healed a blind man who sat begging at the city gate. Perhaps he joined the band of disciples on the dusty road to Jerusalem, 32 km away.

The great Feast of Passover came at the beginning of April and it lasted for a week. It is as important to Jews as Easter is to Christians. At this Feast the Jews remembered how God had delivered them from slavery in Egypt and led them out under Moses.

Passover was the greatest Feast of the whole Jewish year. Jews came from all over Palestine, and from all over the world, to keep the Feast at the Holy City. Jerusalem was packed out. Many Jews had to camp out or, like Jesus and his disciples, lodge in a nearby village. Pilate, the Roman Procurator or Governor, came to Jerusalem, too, for the Passover. Anything could happen in the crowded and excited city. He had to be on the spot to see that order was kept. Perhaps he had another purpose, too. It was the custom at the Feast to release prisoners. This might make him more popular with the Jews.

Palm Sunday

Jesus and his disciples reached Bethany six days before the Passover. Each night of that last week he stayed with his friends there —Mary and Martha and Lazarus.

One night Simon the Leper invited Jesus and his disciples to supper. During the meal Mary showed her great love for Jesus. She had brought a tiny phial of costly perfume called spikenard. She broke it open, and anointed the head of Jesus with its precious drops. Judas Iscariot, who looked after the money for the apostles, was angry to see such waste. "Let her alone," Jesus said to him, "She has anointed my body for burial. Her loving deed will never be forgotten."

Judas must have been very angry when Jesus criticised him in front of all the others. Perhaps he was a proud, clever man and thought that he knew better than Jesus how to bring in the kingdom of God. Perhaps he was just a greedy man. Whatever his reason was, he was ready to betray Jesus for money.

On the first day of the week, our Sunday, Jesus planned his solemn entry into Jerusalem. He sent two disciples on to the village of Bethphage to borrow an ass from a friend. Asses were the most common beasts of burden all through Bible times. They could carry a great deal, they were useful in narrow and crowded streets, and they were not as stupid as we think. Horses were rare. They were used mostly by kings and soldiers. But Jesus was a king of peace and he rode into Jerusalem on a humble donkey. He was fulfilling the prophecy of the Messiah which said, "Behold, Jerusalem, your king comes riding humbly upon an ass."

SPIKENARD

Spikenard was an oil with an exquisite scent. It was made from the roots and leaves of a plant which grows on the slopes of the Himalaya mountains to the north of India. It was rare and costly, and to import it from so far away made it even more costly. The precious drops were kept in small phials made of alabaster. Spikenard was brought by ship up the Red Sea, and then overland by the camel trains of Nabatean merchants.

A WOMAN DECANTING PERFUME

This is from a Roman wall-painting, found in the ruins of a rich man's house in Rome. It dates from the time of Jesus. The daughter of the house is decanting expensive perfume, drop by drop, into an 'alabastron'. This was a tiny jug, with a very narrow neck, made of alabaster. This is the word translated as 'an alabaster box' in the Gospel story of Mary anointing Jesus (Mark 14. 3). By breaking the neck of the phial Mary was able to let the perfume drop on to Jesus' head. It was the custom for guests at a feast to have their heads anointed (see Luke 7.46 and Matthew 6. 17) with cool and refreshing ointment. But the perfume Mary used would have cost the year's wages of a working man.

The disciples threw cloaks over the back of the ass to make a seat for Jesus. The ass picked its way down the hill, across the valley of Kidron, and up the steep climb to Jerusalem. Jesus was surrounded by his disciples and by many other pilgrims from Galilee who knew the popular prophet. They were all excited and happy. "HOSANNA!" they shouted. It was a cry of joy and praise, used in religious processions, and meant SAVE NOW! Some of them spread their cloaks on the road to make a royal way for the Messiah. Others tore leafy branches off the trees by the roadside and made a path with them. As they neared the city, some went in front of Jesus and others behind. It was a gay, cheering little procession.

So Jesus came to Jerusalem, openly fulfilling the prophecy of the Messiah. He was the Saviour, coming to claim his own. But only the faithful pilgrims from Galilee shouted in his honour. His coming seems to have caused no uproar in the busy, bustling, excited city.

Jesus went to the Temple to pray. Then, before dusk, he went back to Bethany for the night. He was safe there from being arrested by the Jewish leaders.

Holy Week

This last week in the earthly life of Jesus is called HOLY WEEK. It began with Palm Sunday.

On Monday Jesus went back to the city and into the Courts of the Temple. Here, for the second time, he fulfilled another prophecy of the Messiah. "The Lord whom ye seek shall suddenly come to his Temple and purify it," said the scripture.

154

A DIARY OF HOLY WEEK

PALM SUNDAY	Jesus rides into Jerusalem	Matthew 21.1-11 Mark 11.1-11 Luke 19.28-44 John 12.12-19
MONDAY	Jesus cleanses the Temple	Matthew 21.12-17 Mark 11.15-59 Luke 19.45-48 John 2.13-17
TUESDAY	Jesus teaches in the Temple	Mark 11.27-33 Mark 12.13-17 Mark 12.41-44 Mark 13.1-2
WEDNESDAY	Judas agrees to betray Jesus	Matthew 26.1-5 and 14-16 Luke 22.1-6
MAUNDY THURSDAY	The Last Supper: Jesus is arrested Trials all through the night:	Mark 14.12-26 Mark 14.27-52 Mark 14.53-72 Mark 15.1-20
GOOD FRIDAY	Jesus is crucified Jesus dies Jesus is buried	Mark 15.21-32 Mark 15.33-41 Mark 15.42-47
SATURDAY *(Jewish Sabbath)*	Jesus in the tomb	Luke 23.54-56
EASTER DAY *(The first Christian Sunday)*	Jesus rises from the dead	John 20.1-10 John 20.11-18 John 20.19-23 Luke 24.13-35

Jesus went into the Outer Court. It was a large and very busy place. It was less sacred than the Inner Courts of the Temple. Gentiles were allowed in the Outer Court, but a big notice warned them that if they went any closer to the Temple they could be put to death. People used it as a short cut, too. Traders set up their stalls there, to sell doves for worshippers to offer as sacrifices. Just outside sheep and oxen were on sale, too, especially at Passover time, when everyone needed a lamb for the Feast. In the Outer Court there were also the tables of the money-changers. Jews had to change their money before they could make their offerings at the Temple. They came from all over the world and they used the money of the country they lived in. Their money might be Roman "denarii," or Greek "drachmas" or "staters", or the local coins of Egypt or Asia Minor. None of these could be used to pay religious dues at the Temple. Only "holy shekels" would do. These were the "staters" of Tyre, the great trading city of Phoenicia. This coin was the only one regarded as holy because it was equal to the old Hebrew coin called a "shekel".

A TYRIAN STATER

This was the coin accepted in the Temple at Jerusalem, because it was the equivalent of the old Hebrew "holy shekel". These were the most common coins in Galilee in the time of Jesus. This one dates from the first century A.D.

156

A ROMAN BANKER

This is a carving on a Roman monument, found in Germany, dating from the third century A.D. It shows the banker at his open-air table. The Jewish money-changers in the Temple court did their business in much the same way.

The money-changers sat at their tables in the open. The Greek word for "bank" ("trapeza") really meant a "table". The changers were licensed by the priests, and the money went to the upkeep of the Temple. There seems to have been cheating, too.

We can imagine the noise and the hubbub which met Jesus when he went into this rowdy Outer Court. He turned over the tables of the money-changers and the stalls of the dove-sellers. He picked up bits of rope, tied them together to make a whip, and drove out the sheep and oxen. "Take these things away!" he cried. "My Father's Temple is a house of prayer—you turn it into a den of thieves!" He was not losing his temper. He was fulfilling the prophecy of the Messiah.

157

The chief priests were furious when they heard of the uproar Jesus had made. They were more determined than ever to arrest Jesus and do away with him. But how could they arrest him? They dare not take him during the daytime when he was surrounded by the crowds. That would cause a riot. And at night time he was nowhere to be found.

On Tuesday, the next day, Jesus again taught in the Courts of the Temple. The religious leaders tried to trap him with difficult questions. Once they demanded, "Tell us—is it right to pay taxes to the Roman emperor or not?" The crowd waited in silence for Jesus to reply. Everyone hated paying taxes to Rome. If Jesus said it was right to pay them, no one would listen to him any more; then the religious leaders could arrest him quietly. But if Jesus said it was wrong to pay them, then they could have him arrested as a rebel against Rome. They had cornered Jesus this time, they thought. "What hypocrites you are," Jesus said. "Fetch me a Roman denarius." Someone went for a Roman silver denarius, for of course no foreign coins were allowed in the Temple. The Roman

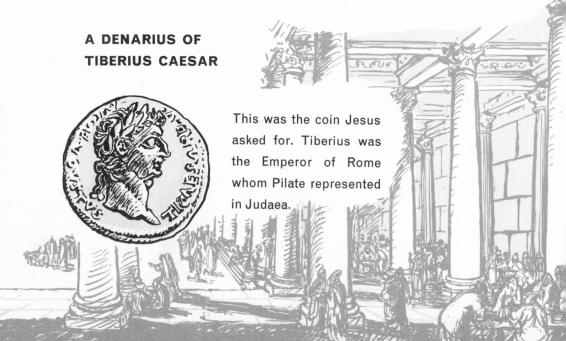

A DENARIUS OF TIBERIUS CAESAR

This was the coin Jesus asked for. Tiberius was the Emperor of Rome whom Pilate represented in Judaea.

denarius had the head of the emperor engraved on it, and that made it a "graven image" which the second commandment of Moses forbade. When Jesus was handed the coin he held it out to the Jewish leaders. "Whose image can you see on this coin?" he asked. "Caesar's," they replied, "Then pay Caesar what belongs to Caesar. And pay God what belongs to God."

Jesus and his disciples sat down opposite the treasury. It had a row of thirteen boxes for the worshippers to put their offerings in. Each one was shaped like a ram's horn. Each horn was labelled to show what the money would be used for—temple dues, bird sacrifices, wood, frankincense, gold for the Holy of Holies. The rest were for free will offerings. The disciples watched as rich men proudly dropped their money into the boxes. They gave a lot of money. Then came a poor widow. She humbly dropped her offering in. It was two tiny bronze coins, the smallest there were. "She has given more than all those rich men", Jesus said. "They have plenty and gave little of it. She has little and she gave it all."

As they left the Temple the disciples said, "Master, look at these huge stones and wonderful buildings." "It will not be long before they lie in ruins," Jesus said. Jesus could see what must happen. It was 40 years after his earthly life that the Jews made their final revolt against the Romans. Jerusalem was besieged and captured and destroyed. Only part of the Temple walls remain today, but they show what a wonderful building it must have been. The stones are about 3.5 m long and 1.2 m high. The heaviest weighs almost 100 tonnes.

The Last Supper

On Wednesday Judas Iscariot went to the chief priests. He offered to betray Jesus to them when he was alone at night – for he knew where Jesus could be found. The chief priests were delighted. They agreed to pay Judas 30 silver staters. That was the price of a slave.

Thursday was the day before the Passover. The evening before the sacred Feast was a time of preparation. The lamb for the Passover meal was offered at the Temple and sacrificed. Supper that evening was another part of the preparation. Then, on the following day, the sacred meal was held with all its solemn ritual. The first three Gospels say that the Last Supper was the Passover meal. John's Gospel says that it was the supper of the evening before. But if that year the Passover fell on a sabbath, Jesus may have brought the sacred meal a day forward. Besides, he knew now that his time was short.

Jesus sent two disciples to prepare for the Last Supper. It was planned secretly. They were to go into the city gate, where they would see a man carrying a pitcher of water, and they were to follow him. This was a secret sign, for it was only women and the despised water-sellers who carried water. The house to which the man led them was the house of Mark who wrote the first Gospel many years later. He was only a lad then. His mother was a disciple of Jesus and she had gladly offered Jesus the guest chamber on the roof of her house.

We can understand why the Last Supper was secretly planned.

160

Jesus was going to do something very important there and he must not be disturbed. If only his most trusty disciples knew where it was to be held he could not be arrested till afterwards. The plan had to be a secret from Judas, most of all.

When evening came Jesus led his disciples up the stone steps outside the house which led to the guest-chamber. Everything was ready for them.

It was the custom for servants or slaves to wash the hot, dusty feet of guests with water. Jesus washed the feet of the apostles himself. "I have given you an example," he said after he had done it, "You must serve others as I have served you."

During the meal Jesus took bread and broke it and shared it among the twelve. "Take and eat," he said, "This bread stands for my body which is going to be given for you." Then he took the cup of wine and passed it round for all to share. "Drink," he said, "This wine is a symbol of my blood which is going to be shed for you. Do this in remembrance of me."

As he gave them the bread and wine Jesus said: "This is the New Covenant. I am making it with my own blood." A COVENANT or TESTAMENT is a BINDING TOGETHER of man and God. The Old Covenant had been made by Moses. It was made with the blood of an animal sacrifice which bound the Jewish people to God. Jesus made a New Covenant or New Testament. He himself was the sacrifice. Through the New, Christian Covenant men may come to God, receive forgiveness, and enter into his family.

For 2,000 years Christians have remembered how Jesus died for them by sharing bread and wine. In doing this they meet with Jesus, their Lord. In doing this they are bound to him and to each other.

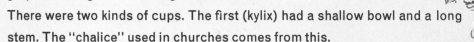

The Bible mentions wine 141 times. It was the usual drink at meals. Water was precious and costly. The red wine of the Jews was made from their own grapes and regarded as the gift of God.

There were two kinds of cups. The first (kylix) had a shallow bowl and a long stem. The "chalice" used in churches comes from this.

Much more common was the deep and rounded cup, and many have been found in Palestine. They were usually made of pottery and sometimes of metal. In wealthy homes they were made of glass. The Last Supper was held in a rich home, where the guest chamber was 'furnished and prepared'. It would have glass drinking vessels. This glass drinking-cup, made in Phoenicia, dates from the time of Jesus. The handles show that it was for drinking. The cup used at the Last Supper may have looked like this, for glass-blowing was a Phoenician art and glass cups were imported from Phoenicia.

THE CUP (Matthew 26. 27)

This silver cup was found at Antioch. It is 19 cm high. The carved openwork shows 12 men and designs of, for example, grape vines (see John 15.1). The two main figures, one on each side, seem to represent Jesus.

But this silver case contains an inner cup, oval in shape. It had been roughly made out of one piece of silver and could hold over four pints of wine.

The inner cup must have been old and sacred, and the silver case made to contain it. Its date is uncertain, perhaps between the third and sixth centuries A.D.

There are many ancient legends about the cup used at the Last Supper—among them the legend of the Holy Grail.

The Chalice of Antioch

At the end of that Last Supper they all sang the Passover Psalms called the HALLEL or PRAISE, Psalms 113 to 118. Then they all went down the stone steps, out of the city, across the brook Kidron, and up the slope to the Mount of Olives opposite the city. Judas knew that Jesus would be going there. John says that he went out during the Last Supper.

Young Mark heard them singing and going down the steps. He followed them in his linen shirt.

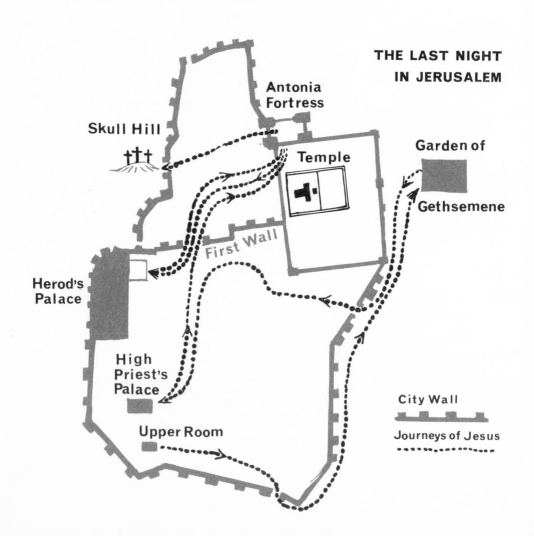

THE LAST NIGHT IN JERUSALEM

Antonia Fortress

Skull Hill

Temple

Garden of

Gethsemene

First Wall

Herod's Palace

High Priest's Palace

Upper Room

City Wall

Journeys of Jesus

The Jewish trials

Jesus led his apostles to a quiet garden called
GETHSEMANE which means OIL-PRESS. There the
olives, from the trees higher up the slope, were pressed to
make olive oil. Olive trees still there today are so ancient that
they may even have been there during the time of Jesus.

Jesus took his three closest apostles with him to a lonely, peaceful
spot. He left them and went a little way forward to pray. He fell on
the ground in great agony of spirit, for he knew the terrible ordeal
he faced. He had to be sure that this was the right way—the will of
God. At last he knew, his prayer was answered, and he was at
peace.

When Jesus came back to the three apostles they were asleep,
and he had to wake them up. Already the twinkling lights of the
soldiers could be seen through the trees.

Judas came up and betrayed Jesus, as he had arranged, with a
kiss of friendship. The servants of the high priest bound him to
lead him away. He gave himself to them freely and ordered his
followers not to resist.

Mark stood near, hiding behind a tree. The soldiers tried to grab
him, catching his linen shirt. But he wriggled out of it and fled
naked in terror. Mark never forgot that night and he wrote about
it in his Gospel.

All the apostles fled, too.

The chief priests had to get Jesus tried and sentenced and put to
death quickly. It had to be all finished before the sabbath began on
Friday at sunset. They had to break many legal customs to do so,
but they did not worry about giving Jesus a fair trial. The only

165

thing that mattered was to get rid of him, and the sooner the better.

Jesus was tried three times during that night. He was all alone. While he was being questioned by the high priest, Simon Peter had crept into the courtyard. He was warming himself with the servants by the fire when someone recognised him as a follower of Jesus. Peter denied having anything to do with Jesus. But his Galilean accent gave him away and twice more he shouted that he did not know Jesus. Then a cock crew, and Peter remembered what Jesus had said—that he would deny him three times before cock-crow. He was heart-broken and went out, weeping bitterly. He never forgot what he had done. He often described it in later years. That was why Mark, his secretary, was able to include the story of Peter's denials in his Gospel.

During the night messengers were hurriedly sent round to bring the members of the Sanhedrin, the Great Council, to the high priest's palace. At sunrise Jesus was brought before the whole Council. False witnesses were brought in to make charges against Jesus, but they did not even agree among themselves. By now the high priest had lost all patience with Jesus. He had not spoken all night—not even to defend himself. "Tell us," he shouted, "Are you the Messiah—the Christ?" "I am," Jesus replied. It was the third time he had openly claimed to be the promised Saviour. "Blasphemy!" cried the high priest, "His own words have condemned him! What is your verdict?" "Guilty!" shouted the Councillors, "Guilty of death!"

There was no need for further witnesses. Jesus had claimed to be the Messiah, and that was blasphemy to those who did not believe in him. The penalty for blasphemy was stoning to death.

166

The Roman trials

The Romans recognised the Great Council as the parliament of the Jews. But they did not allow it to put anyone to death. Only the Roman Governor could pass the death sentence. Now the chief priests had to persuade Pontius Pilate to confirm their sentence and order the execution of Jesus. They knew that Pilate would not care about anyone breaking the religious laws of the Jews. As a Roman he believed in many gods. To him one god was as good as another. So the Jews twisted the charge against Jesus. They accused Jesus of treason against Rome. Pilate could not ignore that.

Early that morning Pilate received the message from the high priest that there was an important prisoner to be tried. Pilate had to act quickly—he had to avoid rioting at all costs. He went from his palace to the Castle of Antonia, the Roman headquarters. Jesus was brought before the Judgement Seat in the courtyard. Pilate soon realised that Jesus was no wild revolutionary. He would not even defend himself. Pilate had a Roman sense of justice. He went out and told the chief priests that Jesus was innocent. He could go free.

The Jewish leaders were furious. "He stirs up the people against Rome from Galilee to Judaea!" they shouted. When Pilate heard that Jesus was a Galilean he saw a way out. Herod ruled over Galilee—let him try Jesus. So Pilate sent Jesus to Herod who was also in Jerusalem at that time. Herod was delighted. He had wanted to see Jesus for a long time. He expected Jesus to perform wonders for him. But Jesus would not say a word. Herod's soldiers mocked Jesus before taking him back to Pilate.

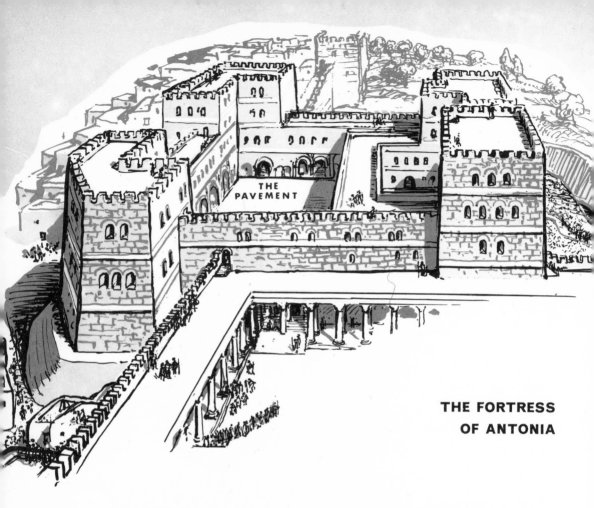

THE PAVEMENT

THE FORTRESS
OF ANTONIA

The fortress had been built at the north-west corner of the Temple at Jerusalem. It was built in Old Testament times to guard the Temple. Herod the Great rebuilt it and named it 'Antonia' in honour of the Roman leader, Mark Antony. It had four high towers of unequal shape. It had a garrison of Roman troops so that they were on the spot to deal with any trouble in the Temple courts. It was the residence of the Roman Governor, Pontius Pilate, when he came to Jerusalem. In the centre was the courtyard or Pavement where Pilate set up his judgement seat (see page 184).

168

WHERE JESUS WAS TRIED BY PILATE

In the middle of the Fortress of Antonia was a courtyard paved with stones.

John's Gospel says that Pilate had his judgement seat in the Pavement (the Greek word means stone pavement) – John 19.13. This paved courtyard, a parade ground for Roman foot and horse soldiers, has been found and is now in the crypt of the convent of Zion.

The King's Game

While Roman soldiers were waiting in the courtyard they played games. They scratched marks for their games on the paving stones. They can still be seen today.

One game called "The King's Game" or "Circle Game", was like our draughts. Each player had four knuckle-bones marked with letters and numbers. As in chess, certain moves had a name – "Alexander's move", "the king's move". The letter B stood for "king" (in Greek "basileus") and it can be seen scratched on the pavement, as well as a royal crown. When the soldiers mocked Jesus as "king of the Jews" they may well have been playing their royal game.

Now Pilate had to decide. Again he talked with Jesus and again he knew that Jesus was no rebel against Rome. He tried hard to avoid sentencing this innocent man to death. But the Jewish leaders were determined to get Jesus executed. They had gathered a great crowd of their followers who did not stop shouting for the death of Jesus.

Pilate had another idea. It was the custom during the Feast to release a convicted prisoner. Everyone knew that a popular criminal named Jesus Barabbas was in prison awaiting death. Pilate went out again to the crowd. "I will keep the custom of the Feast and release one prisoner," he cried. "Which do you want— Jesus Barabbas or Jesus the King of the Jews?" The high priest's followers shouted, "Barabbas!"

"What shall I do with your King?"

"Crucify him!" came the answering shout.

Pilate tried to reason with the crowd. It was useless. Still he hesitated, trying to avoid putting an innocent man to death. Then came a new cry from the high priest's crowd: "If you let this man go you are an enemy of Rome!" Then Pilate was afraid. If he did not give the Jews what they wanted they would make charges against him at Rome. He would be recalled to appear before the emperor and answer them. Already he had offended the Jews on several occasions. This might be the last straw. If he were recalled for trial he might be dismissed. He might even be put to death.

It was either Jesus or himself.

The crucifixion of Jesus
Pilate saved himself. He signed the order for Jesus to be put to death on the cross.

By now it was 6.30 in the morning. A prisoner was always scourged before being put to death. Jesus was flogged with leather whips which had pieces of metal fixed to them. Then the whole company of soldiers gathered round to have fun with him. They dressed him up as a king and mocked him. They made a crown with thorns and thrust it upon his head. They threw a scarlet robe around him. They pushed a reed in his hand to look like a sceptre. Then they pretended to kneel down before him, shouting "Hail! King of the Jews!"

When the soldiers had finished they took away the scarlet robe. They put Jesus' own cloak back on him. They led him out to Skull Hill, just outside the city wall, which was the place of execution. Jesus had to carry the beam of his cross but he kept falling down under its weight. The soldiers ordered a bystander to carry it for Jesus. His name was Simon. He came from Cyrene in North Africa. His two sons, and perhaps Simon, too, became leading members of the Christian church.

THE VIA DOLOROSA
AS IT IS TODAY

The traditional Way of Suffering along which Jesus had to carry his cross out through a city gate to Skull Hill.

THE PLACARD ON THE CROSS OF JESUS

ישוע דנצרת מלכא דיהודאיא

JESVS·NAZARENVS·REX·JVDAEORVM

IHCOYC·O·NAZΩPAIOC·O·BACIΛEYC·TΩN·IOYΔAIΩN

John's Gospel tells us that Pilate himself wrote out a notice to be fixed on the cross of Jesus. It was written in three languages, as in the three lines above —*top*, Hebrew; *middle*, Latin; *bottom*, Greek.
Each line read—JESUS OF NAZARETH THE KING OF THE JEWS.
This is what the placard looked like.
See John 19. 19-22.

Jesus was offered a drug to lessen the pain but he refused it. He was nailed to the cross and it was set upright in a hole in the ground. Two thieves were also crucified, one on each side of Jesus. It was now 9 a.m.

Jesus lived for three hours on the cross. The soldiers, doing guard duty on Skull Hill, diced for his cloak. Weeping women stood near the cross, among them the mother of Jesus. John the apostle was there with her. The rest had fled. Judas had hanged himself, bitterly regretting what he had done.

172

Crucifixions were common in Palestine in Roman times. Passers-by did not linger long. Some of them mocked Jesus. The chief priests came out to mock him, too. Perhaps Barabbas the murderer, now a free man, came out as well.

The Jewish leaders wanted to make sure that Jesus was dead before sunset, when the sabbath began, for a body must not hang on a cross during the sabbath. Pilate gave permission for the three dying men to be despatched. This was done by breaking their legs. When the soldiers came to Jesus they found that he was already dead. He had died at midday.

Two members of the Sanhedrin went to Pilate to get leave to bury Jesus. They were Nicodemus, the Pharisee who came to Jesus by night, and Joseph from Arimathea. They were both secret followers of Jesus. They had not had the courage to speak up for him at the Council meeting.

They had to work quickly to complete their task before the sabbath began at sundown. There was no time to arrange for mourners, or even to embalm the body properly as was the custom. They wrapped the body of Jesus in white linen burial sheets, with some spices between them. They wrapped a separate cloth around his head. Then they laid his body in Joseph's new tomb which had never yet been used. It was cut out of the rock in his garden nearby. The body was laid on a ledge cut in the rock, as was the Jewish custom. Then the great round stone was rolled down the groove cut for it so that it covered the entrance and guarded the tomb.

JEWISH TOMBS

Both these illustrations are of Jewish tombs found near Jerusalem. The one above is the tomb of Herod's family. In ancient times valuables were buried with the dead, and tomb-robbing was common. That was why tombs were guarded. One way of doing this was by a heavy rolling stone. A groove was cut for it in the rock outside the entrance to the tomb. It ran down the groove and covered the entrance. It had to be rolled upwards, and then wedged, before anyone could enter the tomb. With the large stone cylinders used to cover the entrance this was a heavy task for several men.

Tombs were cut in the soft limestone on the side of a hill. A trench was dug in the earth in order to reach a good depth and steps made (A). A low entrance was cut in the limestone and a round stone cut to cover it (B). A first chamber was then cut out (C) to serve as an ante-room, with a ledge all round for mourners. Then the burial chamber (D) was cut out. A niche was cut in the wall (E) and it was on this that the body was laid. Sometimes several niches were cut in the same tomb to provide ledges for several bodies. In time, the remains were buried in the ground to make room for a new burial. But the Gospels say very clearly that the tomb in which Jesus was laid had never been used before (Matthew 27. 60 and John 19. 41).

The resurrection of Jesus

The women disciples from Galilee had watched the burial of Jesus. They saw where the tomb was. They had to leave soon after Nicodemus and Joseph, for dusk was coming on.

The sacred sabbath lasted from sunset on Friday to sunset on Saturday. During that time any kind of work was strictly forbidden. They could do nothing until the sabbath was over. So it was on the first day of the week that they came to the tomb and found it empty. We know that day as Sunday, the sacred day of Christians. Thus, every Sunday is a remembrance of Jesus rising from the dead on the first day of the week.

It was still dark when the faithful women set out for the tomb. They brought spices with them. The last act of love they could do for Jesus was to embalm his body properly. They would wait at the tomb until the gardener or passers-by came to help them roll away the stone.

When they reached the tomb they were astonished. The stone had already been moved away. They hurried back to tell the eleven apostles. Peter and John ran to the tomb as fast as they could. Simon Peter went right inside. The linen cloths lay on the ledge. The burial cloth that had been wound around the head of Jesus lay separately, still rolled up. The body of Jesus had gone. The two apostles did not know what to think as they walked slowly back.

Mary of Magdala remained behind in the garden, weeping. Through her tears she saw the outline of a man who asked her why she was crying. She thought it was the gardener and she pleaded with him to tell her where the body of Jesus had been taken. It was only then, when the stranger spoke her name, that she recognised the voice of Jesus and threw herself at his feet.

That afternoon, Cleopas and his wife, Mary, were going back to their home in the village of Emmaus. It was several miles from Jerusalem in the hill country. They had been disciples of Jesus. But now he was dead and there was nothing to do but to return home. A stranger drew near and spoke with them. When they told him why they were so sad he chided them. He explained to them how the scriptures had foretold that the Messiah must die. When they reached Emmaus they begged him to stay with them for supper. It was while they were eating that Jesus made himself known to them.

They hurried back to Jerusalem to tell the others. While they were still talking about the unbelievable news Jesus appeared among them.

Thomas the apostle was not there that evening. When the others told him that Jesus was alive he would not believe it. "I could only believe it if I saw him and touched him myself," he said. A week later Jesus came again. He told Thomas to feel him and touch him. Then Thomas fell at Jesus' feet and worshipped him.

The ascension of Jesus

For forty days Jesus appeared to his disciples — the GREAT FORTY DAYS, as we call them. Then the time came for him to leave them in body so that he could be with them always in Spirit. He gave them a great work to do—to spread the Good News to all mankind. He promised that he would send his Spirit to them— the Holy Spirit of strength and peace and joy.

Jesus led his disciples up the hill to Bethany. He blessed them

177

there. Then, suddenly, the cloud of the glory of God shone round about him. When it was gone they saw him no more. He had gone back to his heavenly home.

The disciples returned to Jerusalem full of joy. Daily in the Temple they sang praises to God, as other Jews did. But they also met together in the house of Mark's mother, just as they had done when Jesus was with them.

Ten days later came the Feast of Pentecost, the harvest festival of the corn crop. It was also a day of rejoicing for the giving of the Law to Moses on Mount Sinai. The disciples were together in the upper room. The hot morning sun suddenly seemed like fire that set their hearts ablaze. The breeze was like a hurricane blowing new life into them. Suddenly they were filled with the Spirit of Jesus, filled with strength and peace and joy. They rushed out of the house like drunken men and began shouting aloud the Good News of Jesus. That very day 3,000 people were baptised into the name of Jesus. It was the birthday of the Christian Church.

As time went on, this birthday of the Church became a great day for baptism. And because those who were being baptised wore white it became known as "White Sunday". That is why we call it WHIT SUNDAY.

The Church of Jesus began with those few Galilean disciples in Jerusalem. In time it spread over all the earth, taking the Good News of Jesus to men of all nations. It is now nearly 2,000 years old and still, every year, we keep Whit Sunday as the birthday of the Church of Christ.

Passover

Pentecost

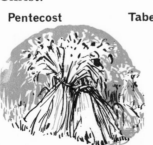

Tabernacle

Dedication

To read

Read these stories of Jesus' travels outside his own land. As you have time, write newspaper reports on them.

In the land of Phoenicia   Matthew 15. 21-28.

At Caesarea Philippi   Mark 8. 27-33.

At Mount Hermon   Mark 9. 2-10.

To research

Although the Samaritans were half-Jews the Jewish people treated them as foreigners, too. Read how Jesus treated them in:

John 4. 5-26; Luke 9. 51-56; Luke 10. 25-37; Luke 17. 11-19. What was different about Jesus' attitude to the Samaritans?

A class study to do

You have been reading about the three great Feasts of the Jewish year and one lesser Feast. The class, divided into groups, can study these Feasts. Each group will produce its own account with drawings and pictures. Reference books will help. The three main Feasts are:

Passover: Exodus 12.3-20. Leviticus 23.5-8; Deuteronomy 16.1-8; Numbers 28.16-25; Luke 22.1-20.

Pentecost: Exodus 34.21-22; Deuteronomy 16.9-12; Numbers 28.26-31; Acts 2.1-4.

Tabernacles: Leviticus 23.34-36; Deuteronomy 16.13-17; John 7. 1-16, 25-31, 37-53.

The lesser Feast is:

Dedication: 1 Maccabees 4.52-59; John 10.22-40.

A story to write

Here are the few references to Nicodemus we are given:
John 3.1-21; John 7.45-53; John 19.38-42.
Joseph of Arimathea is only mentioned in the last of these passages, but legend connects him with Glastonbury in Somerset. Write the story of one of these two men, or both if you wish. Reference books will help.

To imagine

Read the stories of Palm Sunday in Matthew 21.1-11; Mark 11. 1-11; Luke 19.28-44; John 12.12-19. Imagine you were a newspaper reporter in Jerusalem that day. Write an account of it for your paper.

A diary to make

Make a diary of the events of HOLY WEEK, from Palm Sunday to Easter Day. It can be short or long, and you can add your own illustrations if you wish. You can follow Holy Week in Mark's Gospel, beginning at Mark 11.1.

To find out

The first account of the Last Supper is given by Paul in 1 Corinthians 11.23-26. Other accounts are Matthew 26.26-30; Mark 14. 22-26; Luke 22.14-20. These will tell you what Jesus did with the bread and the wine. Find out how the Last Supper is remembered in your own church. Write or tell an account of the service based on it.

A tape-recording to prepare

Make a tape-recording of the trials of Jesus. These are the references:

Jewish Trials: (1) Before Annas, John 18.13; (2) Before Caiaphas, Mark 14.53-65 and Matthew 26.57-68; (3) Before the whole Council, Mark 15.1, Matthew 27.1-2, Luke 22.66-71.

Roman Trials: (1) Before Pilate, Mark 15.1-15; (2) Before Herod, Luke 23.7-11; (3) Before Pilate again, Luke 23.13-25 and John 18.28-19.16.

You can use the words of the Bible or make up your own dialogue.

To read

Read these stories of Jesus appearing to his disciples after he had risen from the dead:

To Mary   John 20.11-28.
To two from Emmaus   Luke 24.13-35.
To some apostles   Luke 24.36-43.
To Thomas   John 20.24-29.
To Peter   John 21.4-17.
The Ascension   Luke 24.50-53; Acts 1.6-11.

Now discuss these questions:

No one expected ever to see Jesus again. What does this show?

Why do you think Jesus only appeared to his disciples?

Suppose some one asked you to prove that Jesus rose from the dead. What answers would you give?

Why do you think Jesus left his disciples in his earthly form?

To examine

Examine the seven sayings of Jesus as he hung on the cross. What can we learn from them?

To discuss

Read the story of Zacchaeus in Luke 19.1-10. Why do you think the tax collector decided to change his whole life?

Meanings to explain

What do the following terms mean:
Fasting; Caesarea Philippi; Great Confession; Peter; Peraea; Tabernacles; Dedication; Hosanna; Holy Week; Covenant or Testament; Hallel; Gethsemane; Sanhedrin; Whit Sunday.

To imagine

Imagine you were young Mark. Describe what happened when Jesus held the Last Supper in your mother's guest-chamber, and when you followed his apostles into the Garden of Gethsemane. Bible references are Mark 14.51-52 and Acts 1.13-14 and 12.12.

To find in your hymnbook

Find hymns in your hymnbook about the events you have read in this chapter: the Last Supper, the Passion or Suffering of Jesus, the Crucifixion, the Resurrection and the Ascension. Read them together in choral speaking and discuss them. How do they help us to understand these great events? Letter in your notebook those you like best, one for each event.

Try writing a hymn yourself about one of them.

First Word
Luke 23. 34

Second Word
Luke 23. 39-43

Third Word
John 19. 25-27

Fourth Word
Mark 15. 34

Fifth Word
John 19. 28-29

Sixth Word
John 19. 30

Seventh Word
Luke 23. 46

THE SEVEN WORDS FROM THE CROSS

To draw or paint

Draw in a series of pictures, as a strip cartoon, the happenings of Holy Week.

Many great artists have painted these events. Find copies of as many as you can and compare them.

Paint one of the great events of Holy Week.

Questions to answer

Why did the religious leaders grow to hate Jesus?

Why did Jesus go into the land of Phoenicia?

Why was it hard for the apostles to understand the kind of Messiah Jesus was?

In what three events did Jesus fulfil prophecies of the Messiah?

Why was the Last Supper planned secretly?

Why did the Jews have to take Jesus to the Roman Governor?

In what ways did Pilate try to avoid sentencing Jesus?

What does Whit Sunday mean to Christians?

Index

Abba, 70
A.D., 53
Amen, 115
Andrew, 101, 102, 118, 122
Anna, 63
Annunciation, 56-7
Antonia, Fortress of, 167, 168
Apostles, 101
Aramaic language, 17, 70, 114, 115
Archelaus, 27, 65
Ark, 40
Asses, 152
Augustus, Emperor, 19, 52, 59, 122
Aureus, 66
Auxiliaries, 27, 31

Bankers, 157
Baptism, 93
Bar Mitzvah, 78
Barabbas, 170
Bartholomew, Nathaniel, 101, 105, 111
B.C., 53
Bedouin, 42, 44
Belladeen, 42, 44
Bethany, 145, 150, 152, 177
Bethlehem, 59
Bethphage, 152
Bethsaida, 102, 104, 118, 122
Bethsaida Julias, 122
Bread, 79, 129
Burial 113, 173-5, 176

Caesarea, 8, 27, 76, 141

Caesarea Philippi, 140-1
Cana, 105, 111
Canaan, 7
Capernaum, 102, 114, 119, 120-3
Carmel, Mount, 8, 76
Carpenter, 67, 74-5
Census, 59
Centurion, 120
Chalice, 162-3
Chinnereth, 13
Chorazin, 34, 124
Christ, 42, 55, 98, 141, 166
Christian Calendar, 53
Christmas, 54, 60
Claudius, Emperor, 66
Cleopas, 177
Cloak, 94
Cooking, 79
Covenant, 161
Cups, 162
Customs office, 123

Dead Sea, 14
Dead Sea Scrolls, 38-41
Decapolis, 14, 15, 124
Dedication 62
Dedication, Feast of, 146
Denarius, 23, 158
Didrachma, 21, 22
Disciples, 100
Distances in Palestine, 46, 127
Doctors of the Law, 34, 83
Dogs, 137, 138-9

Doubting Thomas, 105
Dress, Jewish, 44-5, 67, 94

Edom (Idumea), 25
Education, 70
Elijah, 93, 117, 141, 142
Elizabeth, 57, 91
Emmaus, 177
Epiphany, 65
Esdraelon, Plain of, 10, 11
Essenes, 29, 37-41, 92, 116

Farming, 77, 96
Feeding the 5,000, 128-9
Fellahin, 42, 45, 67
First-born, 62
First-fruits, 21
Fishing, 77, 108-9, 118, 128
Food, 67
Frankincense, 66

Gadara, 16, 124
Galilee, 110
Galilee, Sea of, 12
Gamaliel, 83
Gerasa, 16, 17, 124
Gerizim, Mount, 144
Girding the loins, 45
Gold, 22, 66
Good Friday, 155
Grain, 79, 97
Greek language, 17, 114, 147
Guest chamber, 160, 162

Hazzan, 115

Hebrew language, 17, 70, 115
Hermon, Mount, 12, 76, 140, 142
Herod the Great, 25, 27, 53, 141, 149,
    168
Herod Antipas, 27, 98, 111, 122, 136,
    167
Herod Agrippa I, 103
Herodians, 136
High Priest, 32, 33, 150
Holy Land, The, 7
Holy of Holies, 25
Holy Week, 154-5
Homes, 67-8, 84-5
Hosanna, 154
House-top, 72
Huleh, Lake, 12

Immanuel, 64
Incarnation, 54
Incense Road, 65
Ink, 117
Inns, 58
Isaiah, Book of, 40, 41, 116
Israel, 7

Jacob's Well, 143
James, 101, 103, 118
James the Less, 101, 104
Jericho, 151
Jerusalem, 29, 82, 134
Jesus, The name, 43, 56-7, 62, 71, 83
John, 101, 103, 118, 176
John the Baptist, 14, 39, 57, 90-8, 136,
    141
Joppa, 8

Jordan, River, 12, 13
Joseph, 56, 59, 65, 67, 73, 83
Joseph of Arimathea, 173, 176
Judas Iscariot, 101, 106, 152, 160, 172
Jude, 101, 104

Kidron, Valley of, 99
King's Game, 169

Lamps, 84-5
Last Supper, 160-4
Law, Jewish, 33, 36, 71, 115
Lazarus, 145, 150, 152
Legionary, Roman, 30, 31
Levite, 50
Lights, Feast of, 146
Locusts, 95
Luke, Gospel of, 55, 78, 91

Machaerus, Fortress of, 98
Magdala, 118, 124
Magi, 64-5
Manger, 60-1
Mark, Gospel of, 55, 166
Marriage, 56
Mary, mother of Jesus, 56, 103
Mary and Martha, 145, 150, 152
Mary Magdalene, 124, 176-7
Matthew, Gospel of, 64, 105
Matthew Levi, 24, 37, 101, 105, 122, 123
Maundy Thursday, 155
Mazuzah, 80
Messiah, 42, 55, 93, 98, 100, 125, 129,
    136, 141, 152, 154, 157, 166, 177
Mill-stones, 79

Miracles, 127
Money, 22-3, 66, 156, 157
Moses, 36, 71, 142, 178
Moses' Seat, 34
Myrrh, 66

Nain, 113
Naming, 62
Nazareth, 56, 76, 89, 107, 113, 117
Nazirites, 37, 91
Negev, 10
Nicodemus, 145, 173, 176

Palestine, 7
Parables, 126
Passover Feast, 67, 70, 82, 151, 160
Patriarchs, 101
Paul, 36
Pavement, The, 169
Pens, 117
Pentecost, Feast of, 70, 178
Peraea, 144
Peter, Simon, 55, 101, 102, 118, 122,
    141, 166, 176
Pharisees, 35, 36, 51, 135
Philip, apostle, 101, 104
Philip, ruler, 27, 122, 140-1
Philistines, 8
Phoenicians, 137, 162
Phylacteries, 81
Pigs, 124-5
Play, 71-2
Pontius Pilate, 27, 29, 151, 158, 167,
    168, 170
Priest, 50

Procurators, 27
Publicans, 24
Purple dye, 7

Qumran, 38-9

Rabbi, 34, 82, 83
Rabboni, 34
Roman:
   Census, 59
   Centurion, 120
   Eagles, 28-9
   Empire, 18-9
   Money, 23
   Religions, 19, 20
   Roads, 10
   Soldiers, 27-31
   Taxation, 21, 24

Sabbath, 70, 115, 176
Sadducees, 32, 35, 36, 136
Safed, 111
Salome, 103, 119
Samaria, 143-4
Sanhedrin, 33, 166, 167
School, 70-1
Scribes, 33, 51, 117, 135
Scrolls, 40, 70, 116
Sepphoris, 17, 111, 122
Sharon, Plain of, 8
Shekel, 22, 156
Shema, 80, 115
Shepherding, 77
Sicarii, 37, 101
Sidon, 8, 137

Simeon, 63
Simon of Cyrene, 171
Simon the Zealot, 37, 101, 106
Solomon's Porch, 146
Son of the Law, 78
Sons of Thunder, 103, 118
Spice-mill, 79
Spikenard, 153
Spirit, Holy, 178
Stater, 156, 160
Storms, 128
Sunday, 176
Swaddling, 61

Tabernacles, Feast of, 70, 114-5
Tax collectors, 24, 51
Temple, 37, 99, 146, 147, 148-9, 156-7, 159
Temple-tax, 21, 22, 32, 109
Testament, 161
Thomas Didymus, 101, 105, 177
Tiberias, 122
Tiberius, Emperor, 19, 23, 92, 122, 158
Tithe, 21, 32
Tombs, 124, 125, 174-5
Tools, 74-5
Toys, 71-2
Transjordan, 14
Tyre, 8, 137

Via Dolorosa, 171
Vipers, 95

Way of the Sea, 11, 107
Way of the South, 11

Weaving, 67, 94
Wells, 69
Whit Sunday, 178
Wine, 162
Winnowing, 96-7
Wise Men, 64-5
Wood, 75
Woodworkers, 67, 73, 74-5

Words from the Cross, Seven, 183
Work, 73
Writing, 70, 71, 117

Zacchaeus, 24-5, 151
Zacharias, 91
Zealots, 36-7, 39, 106
Zebedee, 103

ROMANS	JEWS
EMPEROR AUGUSTUS (31 B.C.–A.D. 14) EMPEROR TIBERIUS (14–37)	HEROD THE GREAT (37–4 B.C.) ARCHELAUS HEROD ANTIPAS PHILIP PONTIUS PILATE—GOVERNOR (26–36) KING HEROD AGRIPPA I (37–44)
EMPEROR CALIGULA (37–41) EMPEROR CLAUDIUS (41–54)	
EMPEROR NERO (54–68)	HEROD AGRIPPA II (53–70) FELIX—GOVERNOR FESTUS—GOVERNOR
EMPEROR VESPASIAN (69–79) EMPEROR TITUS (79–81) EMPEROR DOMITIAN (81–96) EMPEROR TRAJAN (98–117)	JEWISH REVOLT: JERUSALEM AND TEMPLE DESTROYED (70) JEWISH REVOLT: 13 JEWS EXPELLED FROM JERUSALEM 13